Natural Law

Natural Law

Reflections on Theory and Practice

JACQUES MARITAIN

Edited and Introduced by William Sweet

ST. AUGUSTINE'S PRESS
South Bend, Indiana

Manufactured in the United States of America.

4 5 6   21 20 19 18 17 16 15

Library of Congress Cataloging in Publication Data
Maritain, Jacques, 1882–1973.
    Natural law: reflections on theory and practice / Jacques
Maritain; edited and introduced by William Sweet.
        p. cm.
    Includes bibliographical references and index.
    ISBN 1-890318-68-X (pbk: alk. paper)
    1. Human rights. 2. Natural law. I. Sweet, William. II. Title.
JC571.M348 2001
171'.2 – dc21   00-012976

∞ *The paper used in this publication meets the minimum requirements of the
American National Standard for Information Sciences – Permanence of Paper
for Printed Materials, ANSI Z39.48-1984.*

ST. AUGUSTINE'S PRESS
www.staugustine.net

Contents

Acknowledgements

Thanks are due to the copyright holder, Jacques Maritain Center, University of Notre Dame, for permission to translate and/or reprint the following essays:

Chapter 1: On Knowledge through Connaturality, from *Review of Metaphysics*, Vol. 4, No. 4 (June 1951), pp. 473-481 [Later published as Chapter 3 in *The Range of Reason*, New York: Scribner's. 1952. pp. 22-29.]

Chapter 2: The Ontological and Epistemological Elements of Natural Law, from: Lecon 1 – *La loi naturelle ou loi non écrite* (compared with Maritain's lecture notes and unpublished manuscripts, by William Sweet). [Portions of this were published as Chapter IV of *Man and the State*, Chicago: University of Chicago Press, 1951, pp. 84-94.]

Chapter 3: Natural Law and Natural Rights, from: Leçon 2 – *La loi naturelle ou loi non-écrite* (compared with Maritain's lecture notes and unpublished manuscripts, by William Sweet) and "The Rights of Man" (Chapter IV of *Man and the State* [1951, pp. 95-107]). [Portions of this appear in "Natural Law and Moral Law" (1952), pp. 65-69; 72-76 in *Moral Principles of Action: Man's Ethical Imperative*, ed. Ruth Nanda Anshen, New York and London: Harper & Brothers, 1952, pp. 62-76, and in Chapter IV of *Man and the State* (pp. 80-84)]

Chapter 4: Natural Rights, from: *The Rights of Man and the Natural Law*, New York: Scribner's, 1943, Chapter 2 – pp. 76-99; 102-114. Reprinted with permission of the copyright holder, Jacques Maritain Center, University of Notre Dame.

Introduction

Jacques Maritain: Life and Thought

1. Life

Jacques Maritain was born on November 18, 1882 in Paris. He was the son of Paul Maritain and Geneviève Favre. Maritain studied at the Lycée Henri IV (1898-9) and at the Sorbonne, where he prepared a *licence* in philosophy (1900-1) and in the natural sciences (1901-2). Although initially interested in the philosophy of Spinoza, he was influenced by a friend, the poet and religious thinker, Charles Péguy, to attend lectures by Henri Bergson at the Collège de France (1903-4), and for a time he was attracted by *bergsonisme*. Maritain received his *agrégation* (having passed the competitive national teaching examinations) in philosophy in 1905.

In 1901 Maritain met Raïssa Oumansov, and they became engaged the following year. The scientism of their teachers had led them to a strong sense of the meaninglessness of life, and both underwent a period of depression. Through the influence of the religious thinker, Léon Bloy, however, they gave up thoughts of suicide. They married in 1904 and were soon thereafter received into the Catholic Church (1906).

Later that year, the Maritains left for Heidelberg, where Jacques continued his studies in the natural sciences. The Maritains returned to France in the summer of 1908. It was at this time that Jacques explicitly abandoned *bergsonisme* and began an intensive study of the philosophy of Saint Thomas Aquinas.

In 1912 Maritain became professor of philosophy at the Lycée Stanislaus, though he undertook to give lectures at the Institut Catholique de Paris. He was named Assistant Professor at the Institut Catholique (attached to the Chair of the History of Modern Philosophy) in 1914, became full Professor in 1921 and, in 1928, was appointed to the Chair of Logic and Cosmology, which he held until 1939.

In his earliest philosophical work, Maritain sought to defend Thomistic philosophy against then-dominant Bergsonian and secular opposition. One of his earliest essays was on "Modern Science and Reason" (1910), and his first book was *La philosophie bergsonienne* [*Bergsonian Philosophy*] (1913). Following brief service in the first world war, the focus of his philosophical work continued to be the defense of Catholicism and Catholic thought (see *Antimoderne* [1922], *Trois reformateurs: Luther, Descartes, Rousseau* [*Three Reformers*] [1925]) and *Clairvoyance de Rome par les auteurs du Pourquoi Rome a parlé (J. Maritain et D. Lallement)* [1929], but Maritain also wrote on topics in logic (*Elements de philosophie II* [*An Introduction to Logic*][1923]) and in aesthetics (e.g., *Art et scholastique* [*Art and Scholasticism*] [1921; 2nd. ed. 1927]).

During the late 1920s, Maritain's interests came to include social issues. He had some contact with the Catholic social action movement, *Action Française*, though he abandoned it in 1927 when it was condemned for its nationalistic and anti-democratic tendencies by the Catholic Church. Still, Maritain's interest in social action remained and, encouraged through his friendships with the Russian philosopher Nicholas Berdiaev (beginning in 1924) and Emmanuel Mounier (from 1928), he began to develop the principles of a liberal Christian humanism and defense of natural rights.

Maritain's philosophical work during this time was eclectic, with the publication of books on Thomas Aquinas (1930), on Religion and Culture (1930), on Christian Philosophy (1933), on Descartes (1932), on the philosophy of science and epistemology (*Distinguer pour unir ou les degrés du savoir* [*The Degrees of Knowledge*] [1932; 8th ed., 1963]) and, perhaps most importantly, in political philosophy. Beginning in 1936, these works include *Humanisme intégral* [*Integral Humanism*], *De la justice politique* (1940), *Les droits de l'homme et la loi naturelle* [*The Rights of Man and Natural Law*] (1942), *Christianisme et démocratie* [*Christianity and Democracy*] (1943), *Principes d'une politique humaniste* (1944), *La personne et le bien commun* [*The Person and the Common Good*] (1947), *Man and the State* (written in 1949, but published in 1951), and the posthumously published *La loi naturelle ou loi non écrite* (delivered in August 1950).

Maritain's work was especially influential in Latin America and, largely as a result of the liberal character of his political philosophy, he came under attack from the left and the right both in France and abroad. For example, travel to Latin America in 1936 led to him being named a corresponding member of the Brasilian Academy of Letters but also to being the object of a campaign of criticism.

Beginning in 1932, Maritain came annually to the Institute of Mediaeval Studies in Toronto (Canada) to give a course of lectures. When he left France for North America at the end of 1939, he decided to stay. Following his lectures in Toronto at the beginning of 1940, he moved to the United States, teaching at Princeton University (1941-2) and Columbia (1941-4). He remained in the United States during the war, where he was active in the war effort—recording broadcasts destined for occupied France—and contributing to the 'Voice of America.' He also continued to lecture and publish on a wide range of subjects—not only in political philosophy, but in aesthetics (e.g., *Art and Poetry* [1943]), philosophy of education, and metaphysics (*De Bergson à St Thomas d'Aquin* [1944]).

In December 1944, Maritain was named French ambassador to the Vatican (serving until 1948), and was actively involved in a number of diplomatic activities, including discussions that led to the drafting of the United Nations Universal Declaration of Human Rights (1948).

In the spring of 1948, Maritain returned to Princeton as Professor Emeritus, though he also lectured at a number of American universities, including the University of Notre Dame and the University of Chicago, and he frequently returned to France to give lectures—particularly in the summer at Soisy. During this time, in addition to his work in political philosophy noted above (as well as *Le philosophe dans la cité* [1960]), Maritain published a number of speculative works on aesthetics (*Creative Intuition in Art and Poetry* [1953]), religion (*Approches de Dieu* [*Approaches to God*] [1953]), moral philosophy (*Neuf leçons sur les notions premières de la philosophie morale* [*An Introduction to the Basic Problems of Moral Philosophy*] [1951]; *La philosophie morale* [*Moral*

Philosophy] [1960]), and the philosophy of history (*On the Philosophy of History* [1957]).

In 1960, Maritain and his wife returned to France. Raïssa died later that year, and Maritain moved to Toulouse, where he lived with a religious order, the Little Brothers of Jesus. During this time he wrote his last book, *Le paysan de la Garonne* [*The Peasant of the Garonne*], published in 1967. In 1970, he petitioned to join the order, and died in Toulouse on April 28, 1973. He is buried alongside Raïssa in Kolbsheim, Alsace, France.

2. Maritain, Natural Law and Natural Rights

The four chapters in this short volume give the reader an introduction to Maritain's views on natural law and natural right. While Maritain wrote a good deal on these topics, particularly in the two decades between 1935 and 1955, in many cases his later work takes up or repeats his earlier writings, sometimes injecting only a few additional words or phrases. (This is particularly evident in those texts used in this volume as Chapters 3 and 4.).

Maritain's natural law theory is a moral theory, and it is part of a tradition of moral philosophy that is one of the oldest known to humanity. Maritain states that there is a universal law that is unwritten, but which all people can know and which all people should respect— a law that both does and ought to serve as a standard for human behaviour. This is 'the natural law.'

As one reads Maritain's writings on natural law and natural rights, it is useful to keep in mind a few basic features of his theory.

To begin with, Maritain would say that his account of natural law is 'Thomistic'—i.e., that it follows the example, and often the letter, of the natural law theory of Saint Thomas Aquinas. There are many instances where Maritain explicitly cites Saint Thomas' views, and Maritain certainly wants to defend Saint Thomas as a philosopher against those who would challenge his moral philosophy—skeptics, relativists, and subjectivists. Nevertheless, Maritain does not follow Saint Thomas uncritically. For example, he gives an analysis of the epistemological side of natural law that he says is rooted in Saint Thomas' view, but which needs to be expanded and developed. What we have, then, is a natural law theory that is Thomistic but also distinctively Maritain's—and which shows a trace of his own early *bergsonisme*.

It is also important to understand what Maritain means by 'law,' when he speaks of his natural law theory. Maritain is not thinking of law in the way in which scientists are seen as presenting laws that govern physical nature as a whole, or in the way in which social scientists speak of 'laws of human behavior.' Nor is the natural law which Maritain describes derivative from, or just analogous to, these kinds of laws. The laws discussed by scientists and social scientists are better seen as generalizations, based on observed particulars. Although they are useful and have a predictive power, they cannot tell us how entities *should* act in the future. Maritain follows Saint Thomas, saying that law is 'an ordinance of reason for the common good made by one who has care for the community and that is promulgated.' This is the *primary* sense of the term 'law'; when the term is applied in science (when we speak of the laws of physics, for example), it is being used in a derivative and analogous sense.

In describing the moral law as 'natural,' Maritain holds that it is natural in two senses. It is natural in the sense that it is related to human nature (i.e., in terms of human functioning and human ends). Because it reflects what it is to be human, and so is common to all human beings because they share the same nature, the natural law has an ontological character. Unlike many modern natural law theories, however, Maritain notes that while the natural law is immanent in and reflects human nature, it is not deducable from human nature.

Maritain also holds that the natural law is 'natural' because of how it is known. It is natural in light of its epistemological—what he calls its 'gnoseological'—character. Maritain notes that we can know things through 'science' or conceptually—for example, by formal reasoning or by empirical observation—but also in a more direct way. The most basic principles or precepts of natural law are not known through reason but 'connaturally' or 'by inclination,' and are indubitable and infallible. This does not mean, however, that the natural law is innate, or that it is like what we today call 'conscience.' Nevertheless, while these basic principles are not known through reason, they are still 'reasonable.'

It is important to distinguish one's knowledge of the natural law from its ontological basis. This distinction reminds us that there can be a natural law—a moral law reflecting the nature of the human person—even if some people do not know it, or even if their awareness of this law is only gradual. It also reminds us of the important role of history and culture in learning moral principles and in moral growth—for we become aware of our inclinations, and human inclinations and moral precepts in general, only over time. Knowledge of natural law is progressive, though the natural law itself does not change or progress.

Some writers draw attention to confusions in natural law theories arising from the sometimes synonymous use of the terms 'natural law' and 'natural right'—the latter term is sometimes used to express the former (e.g., as in, 'I am owed this by natural right'). But Maritain generally avoids this confusion. In the essays in this volume, 'natural right' is the moral power claimed by an individual or by a community in light of the natural law. (See the important footnote 27, giving Maritain's definition of 'right,' in Chapter 3).

Finally, Maritain's moral philosophy provides a clear connection between natural law and natural right. Many recent writers have argued that it is possible to have a political philosophy without an underlying moral philosophy or account of human nature. Maritain certainly agrees that we can—and that we have—come to some consensus about central principles of political philosophy (e.g., human rights) without a metaphysics or a moral theory in the background. Despite the widespread cultural, ideological, and religious differences that existed in the world, the period after the Second World War saw the recognition of a set of rights enshrined in the United Nations Universal Declaration of Human Rights of 1948. Maritain would add, however, that these rights were not authoritative or legitimate because they were the product of an agreement or consensus. There must be—and Maritain holds that there is—a foundation for these rights. This is the natural law. Because of this connection with natural law, and because of his understanding of the 'naturalness' of that law, Maritain is able to defend a view of rights that avoids some of the criticisms of theories of individual rights.

The object of this short volume is to introduce the reader to Maritain's views on natural law and natural rights through his own words.

Chapter 1 gives the reader some of the epistemological background to his natural law theory. In this essay, Maritain reminds us that knowledge through connaturality is not unique to moral knowledge. It is involved in aesthetic experience and in mystical knowledge, as well as in the knowledge of the basic principles of morality.

In Chapter 2, Maritain provides us with a clear statement of what the natural law is, of the two senses in which it is natural, and with his explanation of how we can know that there is such a natural law.

Chapter 3 provides greater detail on the character of the natural law, and explains its relation to other kinds of law that concern human conduct—the eternal law, 'the common law' (or law of civilizations), and the positive law. Specifically, we see why Maritain holds that the latter two have the force of law and can be morally binding. But this Chapter also shows how Maritain is led from a natural law theory to asserting the existence of natural human rights and duties.

In Chapter 4, Maritain provides an enumeration of the rights that he holds follow from his natural law theory. Although written during the Second World War, the list of rights that Maritain provides closely resembles those that came to be explicitly given in the 1948 United Nations Declaration. Importantly, Maritain gives an explanation of what these rights specifically consist in, what moral principles underlie them, what priority exists among rights, and what the conditions for their existence and implementation are. If Maritain's arguments are correct, there is a fairly wide-ranging set of human rights which all human beings should respect.

A Note on the Essays included in this Volume

I have largely followed the standard English editions of Maritain's texts, lightly modifying the translations where appropriate and in light of Maritain's manuscript notes. (I am grateful to M. René Mougel, of the Cercle d'Études Jacques et Raïssa Maritain, Kolbsheim, France, for allowing me access to the Maritain papers during the summers of 1998 and 1999.) I have also slightly altered some of Maritain's references in order to provide more complete or more accurate bibliographical information. These modifications are indicated by being placed in square brackets.

Chapter 1

On Knowledge through Connaturality[1]

Knowledge through connaturality is fundamental to Maritain's account of natural law. In this opening Chapter, we have a presentation of connatural knowledge in general—and we see that it has a place in many kinds of knowledge: poetic (aesthetic), mystical, as well as moral. While connatural knowledge is 'obscure' and not conceptual, it is nevertheless not irrational. Maritain also distinguishes here between moral philosophy, which involves the use of reason, and the knowledge of basic moral principles, which does not. Interestingly, he writes that knowledge through connaturality is of greater validity than discursive knowledge.

I. Saint Thomas and the Notion of Knowledge through Connaturality

THE notion of knowledge through connaturality—that is, of a kind of knowledge which is produced in the intellect but not by virtue of conceptual connections and by way of demonstration—seems to me to be of particular importance, both because of the considerable part played by this kind of knowledge in human existence, and because it obliges us to realize in a deeper manner the *analogous* character of the concept of knowledge. Henri Bergson and William James, who

[1] Paper read at the second annual meeting of the *Metaphysical Society of America*, Barnard College, New York City, February 24, 1951.

were so much concerned, the one with intuition, and the other with experience, never did, I think, bring out and make use of the old notion of knowledge through connaturality. Had they done so, I assume that a number of things would have been clarified in their own teachings. This notion of knowledge through connaturality is classical in the Thomist school. Thomas Aquinas refers in this connection to the Pseudo-Dionysius (*On Divine Names*, Chapter II), and to the *Nicomachean Ethics*, Book X, Chapter V, where Aristotle states that the virtuous man is the rule and measure of human actions. I have no doubt that this notion, or equivalent notions, had, before Thomas Aquinas, a long history in human thought; an inquiry into this particular chapter in the history of ideas—which would perhaps have to take into account such philosophers as Ramanuja, and the Indian school of *bhatki*—would be of considerable interest. I did not embark on such historical research; the question for me was rather to test the validity of the notion of knowledge through connaturality, as elaborated in the Thomist school, and more systematically to recognize the various domains to which it must be extended.

To begin with, I shall refer to a basic distinction made bý Thomas Aquinas, when he explains[2] that there are two different ways to judge of things pertaining to a moral virtue, fortitude for instance. On the one hand, we can possess in our mind moral science, the conceptual and rational knowledge of virtues, which produces in us a merely intellectual conformity with the truths involved. Then, if we are asked a question about fortitude, we shall give the right answer by merely looking at and consulting the intelligible objects

---

[2] *Summa Theologica* [*ST*], II-II, 45, 2.

contained in our concepts. A moral philosopher may possibly not be a virtuous man, and yet know everything about virtues.

On the other hand, we can possess the virtue in question in our own powers of will and desire, have it embodied in ourselves, and thus be in accordance with it, or co-natured with it, in our very being. Then, if we are asked a question about fortitude, we shall give the right answer, no longer through science, but through inclination, by looking at and consulting what we are and the inner bents or propensities of our own being. A virtuous man may possibly be utterly ignorant in moral philosophy, and know as well—probably better— everything about virtues, through connaturality.

In this knowledge through union or inclination, connaturality or congeniality, the intellect is at play not alone, but together with affective inclinations and the dispositions of the will, and is guided and directed by them. It is not rational knowledge, knowledge through the conceptual, logical and discursive exercise of Reason. But it is really and genuinely knowledge, though obscure and perhaps incapable of giving account of itself, or of being translated into words.

Saint Thomas explains in this way the difference between the knowledge of divine reality acquired by theology and the knowledge of divine reality acquired by mystical experience.[3] For the spiritual man, he says, knows divine things through inclination or connaturality, not only because he has learned them, but, as the Pseudo-Dionysius put it, because he suffers them.

As I said at the beginning, knowledge through connaturality plays an immense part in human

---

[3] *ST*, I, 1, 6, ad 3.

existence, especially in that knowing of the singular
which comes about in everyday life and in our
relationship of person to person. Yet it is not with this
everyday practical experience that I shall be concerned
here. For the sake of brevity, I would like only to
outline in a few words its role in some particular typical
fields of human knowledge.

II. Mystical Experience

It is especially with respect to mystical experience, as
witnessed by Christian contemplatives, in whom alone,
according to Bergson, it came to full fruit, that the
Schoolmen developed their theory of knowledge
through connaturality. I shall not dwell on this point,
which is more theological than philosophical. Suffice it
to note that they described mystical contemplation as
grace-given or supernatural contemplation, because
depending both on faith and charity, and on a special
inspiration from God who inhabits the soul. They
observed that obviously a fruitive experience of the
deity cannot be provided by our concepts or ideas,
which, as true as they may be, make us know divine
things at a distance, and through the analogy of
creatures. Consequently, such supra-conceptual
knowledge can come about only through connaturality,
through the connaturality that love of charity, which is a
participation in God's very love, produces between man
and God. The great gnoseological achievement of the
best commentators of Thomas Aquinas, John of St.
Thomas for instance, was to show that in mystical
experience this love grows into an *objective means* of
knowing, *transit in conditionem objecti*, and replaces
the concept as intentional instrument obscurely uniting
the intellect with the thing known, in such a way that

man not only experiences his love, but, through his love, that precisely which is still hidden in faith, the *still more* to be loved, and to be tasted in love, which is the hidden substance of faith. Then, as Saint Thomas puts it, "at the summit of our knowledge we know God as unknown," *tanquam ignotus cognoscitur*, that is, He is known, through love, as infinitely transcending any human knowledge, or precisely as *God*.

* * *

There is, I think, another kind of mystical experience, which, in contradistinction to the one I just mentioned, may be called natural mystical experience; and an example of which we can find in Plotinus and in the classical schools of Indian contemplation. I can only state in a few words the conclusions of a certain amount of research I did on the matter. Here again, to my mind, we have to do with a particular type of knowledge both supra-conceptual and through connaturality. But the connaturality in question here is merely intellectual, and the essential part played by the will consists in forcing the intellect inwards, against the grain of nature, and in obliging it to empty itself of any particular representation. The reality to be experienced is the very Existence, the very *Esse* of the Self in its pure metaphysical actuality—Atman—and as proceeding from the One Self: and it is by means of a supreme effort of intellectual and voluntary concentration, sweeping away any possible image, recollection or idea, any passing phenomenon and any distinct consciousness, in other words, it is through the void that the intellect is co-natured to the unconceptualizable spiritual reality of the thing known.

III. Poetic Knowledge

Another typical instance of knowledge through connaturality appears in Poetic Knowledge. Since German Romanticism and since Baudelaire and Rimbaud, poetry has become self-aware to an unprecedented degree. Together with this self-awareness, the notion of poetic knowledge has come to the foreground. The poet has realized that he has his own way, which is neither scientific nor philosophical, of knowing the world. Thus the fact of that peculiar kind of knowledge which is poetic knowledge has imposed itself upon philosophical reflection. And it would be no use to try to escape the problem by considering poetry a set of pseudo-statements—with no meaning—or a substitute for science intended for feeble-minded people. We must confront in a fair manner the fact of poetic experience and poetic intuition.

Poetic experience is distinct in nature from mystical experience. Because poetry emanates from the free creativity of the spirit, it is from the very start oriented toward expression, and terminates in a word proffered, it wants to speak; whereas mystical experience, because it emanates from the deepest longing of the spirit bent on knowing, tends of itself toward silence and internal fruition. Poetic experience is busy with the created world and the enigmatic and innumerable relations of existents with one another, not with the Principle of Being. In itself it has nothing to do either with the void of an intellectual concentration working against the grain of nature or with the union of charity with the subsisting Love.

Yet poetic experience also implies a typical kind of knowledge through connaturality. Poetic knowledge is non-conceptual and non-rational knowledge; it is born in the preconscious life of the intellect, and it is essentially an obscure revelation both of the subjectivity of the poet and of some flash of reality coming together out of sleep in one single awakening. This unconceptualizable knowledge comes about, I think, through the instrumentality of emotion, which, received in the preconscious life of the intellect, becomes intentional and intuitive, and causes the intellect obscurely to grasp some existential reality as *one* with the Self it has moved, and by the same stroke all that which this reality, emotionally grasped, calls forth in the manner of a sign: so as to have the self known in the experience of the world and the, world known in the experience of the self, through an intuition which essentially tends toward utterance and creation.

IV. Moral Experience

Finally moral experience offers to us the most widespread instance of knowledge through connaturality. As we have noticed, it is in the experiential—not philosophical—knowledge of moral virtues that Thomas Aquinas saw the first and main example of knowledge through inclination or through connaturality. It is through connaturality that moral consciousness attains a kind of knowing—inexpressible in words and notions—of the deepest dispositions—longings, fears, hopes or despairs, primeval loves and options—involved in the night of the subjectivity. When a man makes a free decision, he takes into account, not only all that he possesses of moral science and factual information, and which is manifested to him in concepts and notions, but also all the secret elements of evaluation which depend on what he is, and which are known to him through inclination, through his own actual propensities and his own virtues, if he has any.

But the point on which I should like to lay stress deals with that most controversial tenet in moral philosophy, Natural Law. I don't intend to discuss Natural Law now, I shall only emphasize an absolutely essential element, to my mind, in the concept of Natural Law. The genuine concept of Natural Law is the concept of a law which is natural not only insofar as it expresses the normality of functioning of human nature, but also insofar as it is *naturally known*, that is, known through inclination or through connaturality, not through conceptual knowledge and by way of reasoning.

You will allow me to place myself in the perspective of a philosophy of Natural Law: I do so not in order to assume that you take such a philosophy for granted, but in order to clarify the very idea of Natural Law. My contention is that the judgments in which Natural Law is made manifest to practical Reason do not proceed from any conceptual, discursive, rational exercise of reason; they proceed from that *connaturality or congeniality* through which what is consonant with the essential inclinations of human nature is grasped by the intellect as good; what is dissonant, as bad.

Be it immediately added, to avoid any misunderstanding, first, that the inclinations in question, even if they deal with animal instincts, are essentially human, and therefore, reason-permeated inclinations; they are inclinations refracted through the crystal of reason in its unconscious or preconscious life. Second, that, man being an historical animal, these essential inclinations of human nature either developed or were released in the course of time: as a result, man's knowledge of Natural Law progressively developed, and continues to develop. And the very history of moral conscience has divided the truly essential inclinations of human nature from the accidental, warped or perverted ones. I would say that these genuinely essential inclinations have been responsible for the regulations which, recognized in the form of dynamic schemes from the time of the oldest social communities, have remained permanent in the human race, while taking forms more definite and more clearly determined. But let us close this parenthesis. What are the consequences of the basic fact of Natural Law being known through inclination or connaturality, not through rational knowledge?

First: not only the prescriptions of positive law, established by human reason, but even those requirements of the normality of functioning of human nature which are known to men through a spontaneous or a philosophical exercise of conceptual and rational knowledge are not part of Natural Law. Natural Law, dealing only with regulations known through inclination, deals only with principles *immediately known* (that is known through inclination, without any conceptual and rational medium) of human morality.

Second: being known through inclination, the precepts of Natural Law are known in an *undemonstrable* manner. Thus it is that men (except when they make use of the reflective and critical disciplines of philosophy) are unable to give account of and rationally to justify their most fundamental moral beliefs: and this very fact is a token, not of the irrationality and intrinsic invalidity of these beliefs, but on the contrary, of their essential *naturality*, and therefore of their *greater* validity, and of their *more than human* rationality.

Third: this is so because no conceptual and rational exercise of human reason intervenes in its knowledge of

Natural Law, so that human reason knows Natural Law, but has no part, either in causing it to *exist*, or even in causing it *to be known*. As a result, uncreated Reason, the Reason of the Principle of Nature, is the only reason at play not only in *establishing* Natural Law (by the very fact that it creates human nature), but in *making Natural Law known*, through the inclinations of this very nature, to which human reason listens when it knows Natural Law. And it is precisely because Natural Law depends *only* on Divine Reason that it is possessed of a character naturally sacred, and binds man in conscience, and is the prime foundation of human law, which is a free and contingent determination of what Natural Law leaves undetermined, and which obliges by virtue of Natural Law.

Philosophers and philosophical theories supervene in order to explain and justify, through concepts and reasoning, what, from the time of the cave-man, men have progressively known through inclination and connaturality. Moral philosophy is *reflective* knowledge, a sort of after-knowledge. It does not discover the moral law. The moral law was discovered by men before the existence of any moral philosophy. Moral philosophy has critically to analyze and rationally to elucidate moral standards and rules of conduct whose validity was previously discovered in an undemonstrable manner, and in a non-conceptual, non-rational way; it has also to clear them, as far as possible, from the adventitious outgrowths or deviations which may have developed by reason of the coarseness of our nature and the accidents of social evolution. Eighteenth-century rationalism assumed that Natural Law was either discovered in Nature or a priori deduced by conceptual and rational knowledge, and from there imposed upon human life by philosophers and by legislators in the manner of a code of geometrical propositions. No wonder that finally "eight or more new systems of natural law made their appearance at every Leipzig booksellers' fair" at the end of the eighteenth Century, and that Jean-Paul Richter might observe that "every fair and every war brings forth a new natural law."[4] I submit that all the theories of Natural Law which have been offered since Grotius (and including Grotius himself) were spoiled by the disregard of the fact that Natural Law is known through inclination or connaturality, not through conceptual and rational knowledge.

V. Metaphysics and Knowledge through Connaturality

I think that the critique of knowledge is part of metaphysics, and that the recognition and analysis of that kind of knowledge which is knowledge through connaturality pertain to the object of the critique of knowledge. But knowledge through connaturality has nothing to do with metaphysics itself: metaphysics proceeds purely by way of conceptual and rational knowledge. Like all rational knowledge it presupposes sense experience; and insofar as it is metaphysics, it implies the intellectual intuition of being *qua* being. But neither in this intellectual intuition nor in sense-perception is there the smallest element of knowledge through inclination. In its rational development as in its primal intuitions metaphysics is purely objective. If one confuses the planes and orders of things, if poetic knowledge or mystical experience or moral feeling

---

[4] Heinrich A. Rommen, *The Natural Law: a study in legal and social history and philosophy* (St. Louis: Herder, c1947), p. 106.

claim to become philosophical knowledge, or if a philosophy which despairs of reason tries to capture those kinds of knowledge through connaturality, and to use them as an instrument—everyone loses his head, knowledge through inclination and metaphysics are simultaneously spoiled.

Chapter 2

The Ontological and Epistemological Elements of Natural Law[5]

In this Chapter, Maritain describes the 'naturalness' of natural law, by appealing to arguments defending it as both ontologically (i.e., metaphysically) and gnoseologically (i.e., epistemologically) natural. Metaphysically, natural law is immanent in human nature and, because human nature has a teleological dimension, it is in terms of the 'normality of the functioning' of human beings that we can know what they should do. Epistemologically, moral knowledge is not innate, but through self-awareness and the experience of living we can acquire connaturally the knowledge of the basic principles of the natural law. Moral knowledge, then, occurs in time and in a social world, but it does not follow that it is reducible to historical accident or is just social practice.

I. Introduction

The authentic idea of natural law is an inheritance of Greek and Christian thought. This idea has its origin,

---

[5] From *La loi naturelle ou loi non écrite*, Fribourg (Suisse): Éditions universitaires, 1986, leçon 1, pp. 19-35; edited, compared with earlier translations, and revised by William Sweet. Parts of Chapter IV of *Man and the State* (Chicago: University of Chicago Press, 1951, pp. 84-94) and of *The Rights of Man and Natural Law* (New York: Scribner's, 1943, pp. 59-61; 62-4), follow this lecture very closely. Where the corresponding sections of *Man and the State* include additional material that is useful, I have incorporated it here, and enclosed it in square parentheses.

not in Grotius—who, although he is considered to be the father of 'natural law theory,' in fact began by deforming it—but, long before him, in Francisco de Vitoria and Suarez; and further back, in Saint Thomas Aquinas. He alone among these great authors grasped the matter of the natural law and made it into a wholly consistent doctrine. Following him, we see a process of degeneration caused by the misunderstanding of certain elements of the concept of natural law. [...]

In order to discover the true origin of the idea of natural law, we have to go back to Saint Augustine, to the Church Fathers, to Saint Paul, and even further back to Cicero, to the Stoics, to the great moralists of antiquity and its great poets, particularly Sophocles. Antigone is the heroine of natural law; she was aware of the fact that, in transgressing the human law and being crushed by it, she was obeying a higher commandment—that she was obeying laws that were unwritten, and that had their origin neither today nor yesterday, but which live always and forever, and no one knows where they have come from.[6]

---

[6] ["Nor did I deem
Your ordinance of so much binding force,
As that a mortal man could overbear
The unchangeable unwritten code of Heaven;
This is not of today and yesterday,
But lives forever, having origin
Whence no man knows: whose sanctions I were loath
In Heaven's sight to provoke, fearing the will
Of any man."
(Sophocles, *Antigone*, ii. 452-60, [From: *The Dramas of Sophocles rendered in English Verse, Dramatic and Lyric*, by Sir George Young, bart. Cambridge: Deighton, Bell and Co.;

If we want to go deeper into the analysis of natural law, we must distinguish two elements: an ontological element and a gnoseological element.

II. The First Element in Natural Law: the Ontological Element

I am taking it for granted that there is a human nature, and that this human nature is the same in all men. I am taking it for granted that we also admit that man is a being gifted with intelligence, and who, as such, acts with an understanding of what he is doing, and therefore with the power to determine for himself the ends which he pursues. On the other hand, possessed of a nature, or an ontological structure which is a locus of intelligible necessities, man possesses ends which necessarily correspond to his essential constitution and which are the same for all. All pianos [whatever their particular type and in whatever spot they may be] have as their end the production of musical sounds. If they do not produce these sounds, they must be tuned, or discarded as worthless. But since man is endowed with intelligence and determines his own ends, it is up to him to put himself in tune with the ends necessarily demanded by his nature. This means that there is, by the very virtue of human nature, an order or a disposition which human reason can discover and according to which the human will must act in order to attune itself to the essential and necessary ends of the human being. The unwritten law, or natural law, considered in its ontological aspect, is nothing more than that [...].

The example that I just used—taken from the world of human workmanship—was purposely crude and

London: G. Bell and Sons, 1888.])]

provocative: yet did not Plato himself have recourse to the idea of any work of human art whatever, the idea of Bed, the idea of Table, in order to make clear his theory of eternal Ideas? What I mean is that every being has its own natural law, just as it has its own essence. I have used the example of something produced by human industry because this kind of example is easier (though at the same time it is more vexing); everything produced by human industry has its own natural law, that is, has a normal way of functioning—the proper way in which, by reason of its specific construction, it demands to be put into action [and that says how it *"should"* be used]. Confronted with any supposedly unknown gadget, be it a corkscrew or a top or an atomic bomb, children as much as scientists, in their eagerness to discover how to use it, look for the law specific to that object, without ever questioning the existence of that inner law.

The same applies for natural objects. Any kind of thing existing in nature, a plant, a dog, a horse, has its own natural law, that is, the normality of its functioning, the proper way in which, by reason of its specific structure and specific ends, it should achieve fulness of being either in its growth or in its behaviour. [Washington Carver, when he was a child and healed sick flowers in his garden, had an obscure knowledge, both by intelligence and congeniality, of that vegetative law of theirs.] Horse-breeders have an experiential knowledge, both by intelligence and congeniality, of the natural law of horses, a natural law with respect to which a horse's behaviour makes him a *good horse* or a *vicious horse* in the herd. Well, horses do not enjoy free will, their natural law is but a part of the immense network of essential tendencies and regulations involved in the movement of the cosmos. The horse who fails in that equine law only obeys the universal order of nature on which the deficiencies of his individual nature depend. If horses were free, there would be an ethical or moral way of conforming to the specific natural law of horses. But a horsy morality is a dream because horses are not free. The natural law of all beings existing in nature is the proper way in which, by reason of their specific nature and specific ends, they *should* achieve fulness of being in their behaviour. This very word *should* had only a metaphysical meaning (as when we say that a good or a normal eye "should" be able to read letters on a blackboard from a given distance.) The same word *should* starts to have a moral meaning, that is, to imply moral obligation, when we pass the threshold of the world of free agents. In a sense, a natural law may be found in all beings. For man, the natural law is a moral law because man obeys or disobeys it freely, not necessarily, and because human behaviour pertains to a particular, privileged order which is irreducible to the general order of the cosmos and tends to a final end superior to the immanent common good of the universe.

The first basic element to be recognized in natural law is, then, the *ontological* element; I mean the *normality of functioning* which is grounded on the essence of that being: man. Natural law in general [as we have just seen] is the ideal formula of development of a given being. It might be compared with an algebraical equation according to which a curve develops in space [, yet with man the curve has freely to conform to the equation]. Let us say, then, that in its ontological aspect, natural law is an *ideal order* relating to human actions, a divide between the suitable and the unsuitable, between what is proper and what is improper to the ends of human nature or essence. This is an ideal order or divide which is rests on human nature or essence and the unchangeable necessities rooted in it.

Let me make a short parenthetical remark. I do not mean that the proper regulation for each possible human situation is contained in the human essence, as Leibniz believed that every event in the life of Caesar was contained beforehand in the idea of Caesar. Human situations are something existential. Neither they nor their appropriate regulations are contained in the essence of man. I would say that they ask questions of that essence. Any given situation, for instance the situation of Cain with regard to Abel, implies a relation to the essence of man, and the possible murder of the one by the other is incompatible with the general ends and innermost dynamic structure of that rational essence. [It is rejected by it.] Hence the prohibition of murder is grounded on the essence of man and required by it, and the precept "thou shalt not kill" is a precept of natural law. Because a primordial and most general end of human nature is to preserve being—the being of that existent who is a person, and a universe unto himself [; and because man insofar as he is man has a right to live].

Suppose a completely new case or situation, for instance, what we now call *genocide* (which is not as new as the word). In line with what I have just said, the behaviour of "putting to death a race or a human community as such" is something that will strike the human essence as incompatible with its general ends and innermost dynamic structure: that is to say, it will just see that genocide is prohibited. [The condemnation of genocide by the General Assembly of United Nations[7] has sanctioned the prohibition of the crime in

---

[7] [December 11, 1948.]

question by natural law—] which does not mean that
that prohibition was part of the essence of man, as a
metaphysical feature eternally inscribed in it, nor that it
was a notion recognized from the start by the
conscience of humanity. [...]
   To sum up, let us say that natural law is something
both *ontological* and *ideal.* It is something *ideal,*
because it is grounded on the human essence, on its
unchangeable structure and the intelligible necessities it
involves. On the other hand, natural law is something
ontological, because the human essence is an
ontological reality, which moreover does not exist
separately, but in every human being, so that by the
same token natural law dwells as an ideal order in the
very being of every existing man.
   In that first consideration, or with regard to the basic
ontological element it implies, natural law is
coextensive with the whole field of natural moral
regulations, the whole field of natural morality.
Whatever we can or might say about rights and duties,
about virtues, or about the moral obligations of human
beings, this only expresses the 'normality of
functioning' of which we have spoken. And so, not only
the primary and fundamental regulations but the
slightest regulations of natural ethics mean conformity
to natural law—even the natural obligations or rights of
which we perhaps have now no idea, and of which men
will become aware in a distant future.
   An angel who knew the human essence in his
angelic manner and all the possible existential
situations of man, would know natural law in the
infinity of its extension. But we do not, though the
Eighteenth Century theoreticians believed they did. [...]

III. The Second Element in Natural Law: the Gnoseological Element

The second basic element contained in the natural law— I mean, the natural law *as known,* and thus as measuring in actual fact human practical reason, which is the measure of human acts—is not the ontological element (i.e., the normality of its functionning), but the gnoseological element.

Natural law is not a law written by men. Men know it with greater or less difficulty, and in different degrees, running the risk of error here as elsewhere. The only practical knowledge all men have naturally and infallibly in common, as a self-evident principle, intellectually perceived by virtue of the concepts involved, is that we must do good and avoid evil. This is the preamble and the principle of natural law; it is not the law itself. Natural law is the ensemble of things to do and not to do which follow therefrom in a *necessary* fashion. That every sort of error and deviation is possible in the determination of these things merely proves that our sight is weak, our nature coarse, and that innumerable accidents can corrupt our judgment. Montaigne remarked that, among certain peoples, incest and thievery were considered virtuous acts. Pascal was scandalized by this. All this proves nothing against natural law, any more than a mistake in addition proves anything against arithmetic [, or the mistakes of certain primitive peoples, for whom the stars were holes in the tent which covered the world, prove anything against astronomy].

By the very fact that the Natural law is an unwritten law, man's knowledge of it has increased little by little as man's moral conscience has developed. The latter

was at first in a twilight state.[8] Anthropologists have
taught us within what structures of tribal life and in the
midst of what magic this knowledge of the natural law
was awakened, and how it was primitively formed. This
shows simply that the knowledge men have had of the
unwritten law has passed through more diverse forms
and stages than certain philosophers or theologians have
believed. At the same time, we become aware of the
fact that the knowledge which our own moral
conscience has of this law is doubtless still imperfect,
and very likely it will continue to develop and to
become more refined as long as humanity exists. Only
when the Gospel has penetrated to the very depth of
human substance will natural law appear in its flower
and its perfection.

[So the law and the knowledge of the law are two
different things.] Yet the law has force of law only
when it is promulgated. It is only insofar as it is known
and expressed in assertions of practical reason that
natural law has force of law. The gnoseological element
is therefore fundamental in natural law.

It is important to recognize that human reason does
not discover the regulations of natural law in an abstract
and theoretical manner, as a series of geometrical
theorems. Moreover, it does not discover them through
the conceptual exercise of the intellect, or by way of
rational knowledge. I think that the teaching of St
Thomas here should be understood in a much deeper
and more precise fashion than is usual. When he says
that human reason discovers the regulations of natural
law through the guidance of the *inclinations* of human
nature, he means that the very mode or manner in which

---

[8] Cf. Raissa Maritain, *Histoire d'Abraham ou les premiers âges
de la conscience morale* (Paris: Desclée de Brouwer. 1947).

human reason knows natural law is not rational knowledge, but knowledge *through inclination.*

Saint Thomas largely developed this notion of knowledge by inclination, but elsewhere—in the *Summa theologiae*, II-II, 45, 2.[9] Knowledge by inclination or by connaturality is a kind of knowledge that is not clear, like that obtained through concepts and conceptual judgments. It is obscure, unsystematic, vital knowledge,

---

[9] [This is, in my opinion, the real meaning implied by Saint Thomas, even though he did not use the very expression when treating of Natural Law. Knowledge through inclination is generally understood in all his doctrine on Natural Law. It alone makes this doctrine perfectly consistent. It alone squares with such statements as the following ones: "Omnia illa ad quae homo *habet naturalem inclinationem, ratio naturaliter apprehendit ut bona,* et per consequens ut opere prosequenda; et contraria eorum, ut male et vitanda" (*ST* I-II, 94. 2), "Ad legem naturae pertinet omne illud ad quod homo inclinatur secundum naturam. [...] Sed, si loquamur de actibus virtuosis secundum seipsos, prout scilicet in propriis speciebus considerantur, sic *non* omnes actus virtuosi sunt de lege naturae. Multa enim secundum virtutem fiunt *ad quae natura non primo inclinat; sed per rationis inquisitionem ea homines adinvenerunt,* quasi utilia ad bene vivendum (*ST* I-II, 94. 3). The matter has been somewhat obscured because of the perpetual comparison that Saint Thomas uses in these articles between the speculative and the practical intellect, and by reason of which he speaks of the *propria principia* of Natural Law as *"quasi conclusiones principiorum communium"* (*ST* I-II, 94. 4). As a matter of fact, those *propria principia* or specific precepts of Natural Law are in no way conclusions rationally deduced; they play in the practical realm a part similar to that of conclusions in the speculative realm. (And they appear as inferred conclusions to the "after-knowledge" of the philosophers who have to reflect upon and explain the precepts of Natural Law.) [This note appears only in *Man and the State.* Ed.]]

by means of instinct or sympathy, and in which the intellect, in order to make its judgments, consults the inner leanings of the subject—the experience that he has of himself—and listens to the melody produced by the vibration of deep-rooted tendencies made present in the subject. All this leads to a judgment—not to a judgment based on concepts, but to a judgement which expresses simply the conformity of reason to tendencies to which it is inclined. [...]

When one has clearly seen this fact, and when, moreover, one has realized that Saint Thomas' views on the matter call for an historical approach and a philosophical enforcement of the idea of development that the Middle Ages were not equipped to carry into effect, then one is able to have a completely comprehensive concept of Natural Law. And one understands that the human knowledge of natural law has been progressively shaped and molded by the inclinations of human nature, starting from the most basic ones. We should not expect philosophy to offer us an *a priori* picture of those genuine inclinations [which are rooted in man's being as vitally permeated with the preconscious life of the mind, and] which either developed or were released as humanity advanced. They are evinced by the very history of human consciousness. Those inclinations were really genuine which, in the immensity of the human past, have guided reason in becoming aware, little by little, of the regulations that have been most definitely and most generally recognized by the human race, starting from the most ancient social communities. For the knowledge of the primordial aspects of natural law was first expressed in social patterns rather than in personal judgments. This knowledge has developed from inside, within the double

protecting tissue of human inclinations and human
society.

With regard to the second basic element, the
gnoseological element which natural law implies in
order to have force of law, we can say that natural
law—that is, natural law *naturally known,* or, more
exactly, natural law *the knowledge of which is embodied
in the most general and most ancient heritage of
humanity*—covers only the field of the ethical
regulations of which men have become aware by virtue
of knowledge through inclination, and which are the
basic or first *principles* of moral life—progressively
recognized from the most common principles to the
more and more specific ones. This is to put together two
perspectives which, at first glance, appear
contradictory: the first perspective sees the natural law
as coextensive with human nature, so that every ethical
regulation that might be discovered may be found to be
in agreement with this 'normality of the functionning of
human nature'; the other perspective does not deal with
the entire set of moral regulations, but only with the
very first principles (because it focuses not so much on
the ontological element as on the gnoseological
element, and because it deals only with those
regulations that are known by inclination). [...]

All these previous remarks may help us to
understand why, on the one hand, a careful examination
of the data of anthropology would show that the
fundamental *dynamic schemes* of natural law, if they are
understood in their authentic, that is, still undetermined
meaning (for instance: to take a man's life is not like
taking another animal's life; or, the family group has to
comply with some fixed pattern; or, sexual intercourse
has to be contained within given limitations; or, we are
bound to look at the Invisible; or, we are bound to live

together under certain rules and prohibitions), are subject to a much more universal awareness—everywhere and in every time—than would appear to a superficial glance; and why, on the other hand, an immense amount of relativity and variability is to be found in the particular rules, customs, and standards in which, among all peoples of the earth, human reason has expressed its knowledge even of the most basic aspects of natural law: for, as I pointed out above, that spontaneous knowledge does not bear on moral regulations conceptually discovered and rationally deduced, but on moral regulations known through inclination, and, at the start, on general tendential forms or frameworks, I just said on *dynamic schemes* of moral regulations, such as can be obtained by the first, "primitive" achievements of knowledge through inclination. And in such tendential frameworks or dynamic schemes many various, still defective contents can occur,—not to speak of the warped, deviated, or perverted inclinations which can mingle with the basic ones.

We may understand at the same time why natural law essentially involves a dynamic development, and why moral conscience, or the knowledge of natural law, has progressed from the age of the cave-man in a double manner: first, as regards the way in which human reason has become aware in a less and less crepuscular, rough, and confused manner, of the primordial regulations of natural law; second, as regards the way in which it has become aware—always by means of knowledge through inclination—of its further, higher regulations. And such knowledge is still progressing, it will progress as long as human history endures. That progress of moral conscience is indeed the most unquestionable instance of progress in humanity.

I have said that natural law is unwritten law: it is unwritten law in the deepest sense of that expression, because our knowledge of it is no work of free conceptualization, but results from a conceptualization *bound* to the essential inclinations of being, of living nature, and of reason, which are at work in man, and because it develops in proportion to the degree of moral experience and self-reflection, and of social experience also, of which man is capable in the various ages of his history. Thus it is that in ancient and mediaeval times attention was paid, in natural law, to the *obligations* of man more than to his *rights*. The proper achievement—a great achievement indeed—of the XVIIIth Century has been to bring out in full light the *rights* of man as also required by natural law. That discovery was essentially due to a progress in moral and social experience, through which the root *inclinations* of human nature as regards the rights of the human person were set free, and consequently, *knowledge through inclination* with regard to them developed. But, according to a sad law of human knowledge, that great achievement was paid for by the ideological errors, in the theoretical field, that I have stressed at the beginning. Attention even shifted from the obligations of man to his rights only. A genuine and comprehensive view would pay attention *both* to the obligations and the rights involved in the requirements of natural law.

Chapter 3

Natural Law and Natural Rights

*In the selections in this Chapter, we see that while natural law is universal, it is not the only type of law that can be morally binding on human beings. The Chapter begins with Maritain's explanation of the relation among the different kinds of 'law'— the eternal law, the natural law, the 'common law' (or law of civilizations), and the positive law—and how it is that the latter two can be binding on conscience. Maritain then proceeds to show how a natural law theory leads to the recognition of natural rights, but distinguishes his view from social contract theories which hold that individual rights are of ultimate importance. While rights have a fundamental value (because they are grounded in the natural law), Maritain reminds us that we must not forget their relation to the common good. Maritain's distinction between the person and the individual, elaborated in his short book, **The Person and the Common Good** (1947), bears on the limits of individual rights in relation to the common good, but also on the importance of the rights of the person over the common good of the community.*

I. Natural Law and the Eternal Law[10]

[[T]he concept of Natural Law is given its definitive meaning only when that of Eternal Law has been established.]

---

[10] [From *La loi naturelle ou loi non écrite*, Fribourg (Suisse): Editions universitaires, 1986, leçon 2, pp. 37-8; 40-3; edited, compared with earlier translations, and revised by William Sweet. Parts of Maritain's essay, "Natural Law and Moral Law" [in *Moral Principles of Action: Man's Ethical Imperative*, ed. Ruth Nanda Anshen (New York and London: Harper & Brothers, 1952), pp. 65-69], follow this lecture closely. Where

This concept of Eternal Law is not solely theological. In the *Summa theologiae*, Saint Thomas insisted on the existence of the eternal law on the basis of theological arguments, but it is a philosophical truth as well, one which the philosopher with his means alone can reach and establish. God exists. He is the first cause of being, activating all beings. It is by his intellect and will that he acts: from which we have the notion of Providence. The entire community of the universe is governed by the divine reason. Hence there is in God, as in one who governs the entirety of created beings, this very reality which is the judgment and command of the practical reason applied to the governing of a unified community: in other words, this very reality which we call *law*. Eternal Law is one with the eternal wisdom of God and the divine essence itself. Saint Thomas defines this Eternal Law as "nothing other than the exemplar of divine wisdom insofar as this wisdom directs all the actions and movements of things ."[11]

It is evidently to this Eternal Law that we must have recourse if we are in search of the first foundation of Natural Law. Because every law is a work of reason, at the source of Natural Law there must be reason: not human reason but Subsistent Reason, the Intelligence which is one with the First Truth itself; there we have the Eternal Law. [...] Saint Thomas explains in article 2 of question 91 that "Law is a measure and a rule, and hence is found in him who rules, and also in that which is measured and ruled, for a thing is ruled and measured insofar as it participates in the measure and rule existing in the one who rules. Now, since all things are ruled and measured by the Eternal Law, we must

---

this latter essay includes additional material that may be useful, I include it here, and enclose it in square parentheses.]

[11] *ST* I-II, 93, 1.

conclude that they participate in this Law insofar as they derive from it the inclinations through which they tend naturally toward their proper operations and ends"—this is a notion of the natural law considered both in its ontological element and as a whole. Let us turn now from this still very general notion to one that focuses on rational nature in particular. We should note that, among all creatures, the rational creature is subject to divine providence in a particular way—a "more excelient way," Saint Thomas writes— inasmuch as it has a share in providential government, by being provident both for itself and others. "Thus the rational creature by its very rationality participates in the eternal reason, and because of this participation has a natural inclination to the actions and ends proper to it"—inclinations of knowledge; rational and intellectual inclinations. Here we find a number of notions confused together. We have those inclinations which proceed from human nature, *qua* human, inclinations rooted in reason, according to which human reason judges what is good and what is bad. The principal feature of article 2 of question 91 is the following: in this creature, there is a participation in the eternal law according to which it possesses a natural inclination to act in a certain way and towards the end to which it is suited. "It is this participation in the Eternal Law enjoyed by the rational creature which is called the Natural Law." All beings participate in the eternal law: in this sense, there is a natural law for all beings. But when it concerns the rational creature, we have a [specific] concept of the natural law. [...] All that is good and all that is evil is only an impression of the divine light in us. "Thus it is clear that the natural law is nothing other than a participation of the eternal law in the rational creature." If we turn to article 4, question 19, of the *Prima secundae* [of the *Summa theologiae*], we see that the goodness of the human will, which depends on reason, looking at natural law as its immediate measure, depends all the more on the eternal law, which is the divine reason. In fact, secondary causes act only in the virtue of the first cause, which activates them. Now the very property that human reason possesses of being the rule and the measure of the human will—a rule by which the goodness of the will is constituted and measured—this very property of human reason arises from eternal law, which is divine Reason. Hence it is manifest that the goodness of the human will depends much more on Eternal Law which is the Divine Reason than on Human Reason [or Natural Law]. And there where human reason is defective, we must have recourse to eternal reason. [...]

We must go further. We must recognize that the natural law, and the authority of reason as the form and measure of human acts, are not simply rooted in God or guaranteed by God (as every active faculty or power of creatures is) but—and this seems to me to be very important—the divine reason alone is the author of natural law, and natural law emanates from it. [It alone causes that Law to exist, and it alone causes it to be known, insofar as it is the cause of human nature and of its essential inclinations.] It is not merely a matter of saying that the divine reason guarantees the value and the exercise of our own reason (which was the dominant view after Saint Thomas [and generally held in the sixteenth and seventeenth centuries)]—that God guarantees the exercise and value of our reason as though it were our reason which instituted Natural Law, or at least deciphered it in nature and made it known by its own effort and authority. Let us say rather that here the divine reason is *the only reason* to be considered. The law, in effect, is essentially an ordinance of reason (*ordinatio rationis*), so that without an ordering reason there is no law. The notion of law is essentially bound up with that of an ordering reason. Indeed, in the case of Natural Law, human reason has no share in the initiative and authority establishing the Law, either in making it exist or in making it known.

The fact that the divine reason is the only reason which is author of the Law enables us to understand better the meaning of Saint Thomas' expression: 'Natural Law is a participation in the Eternal Law. It is the divine reason which is involved.' If human reason had a hand in it, the Law would, to that extent, have no more than the value of human authority. [...]

The formal medium by which we advance in our knowledge of the regulations of Natural Law is not the conceptual work of reason, but rather those inclinations to which the practical intellect conforms in judging what is good and what is bad. Through the channel of natural inclinations the divine reason imprints its light upon human reason. This is why the notion of knowledge through inclination is basic to the understanding of Natural Law, for it brushes aside any intervention of human reason as a creative factor in Natural Law. [...]

II. The Analogical Character of the Notion of Law[12]

The concept of law is an analogous concept.

---

[12] [From *La loi naturelle ou loi non écrite*, Fribourg (Suisse): Editions universitaires, 1986, leçon 2, pp. 44-6.]

In article 4, question 90, of the *Prima secundae,* Saint Thomas gives us a general definition of law: "a certain ordinance of reason for the common good, promulgated by him who has the care of the community." The definition of Saint Thomas is expressed only in terms of intelligence and reason, not will. Will is not involved in the definition—in order to kill, it is not a matter of having the will to kill. The will is involved [in law] only because there is no 'order' without some presence of it. That which defines law is reason, intelligence, because there is an order. It is reason that can make order, and which is itself order. Law presupposes an ordination of reason for the common good. The community, then, is the subject of the law, while the good of this community is the end or purpose of the law. The law is promulgated by the person who has care for the community because, without this, he would not have the authority to make law. It is only so far as one is responsible for the community—charged with promoting its common good—that he has a God-given authority allowing him to make a law or to establish an order that can be [legitimately] imposed on others.

It should be noted, concerning Natural Law, that the very word "law" risks being misunderstood because the most obvious and the most immediate notion that we have of law is that of written law or positive law: consequently, if we overlook the analogical character of the notion of law, we run the risk of conceiving Natural Law and every species of law after the pattern of the type of law best known to us—the written law.

Now the very notion of the Eternal Law seems to me to illuminate this analogical character of law. God is not a legislator like others. The community that he heads is the entire created universe. The Eternal Law is not written upon paper; it is promulgated in the divine intellect and is known in itself solely by God and by those who see him in his essence. However, Saint Thomas writes, every rational creature knows a certain reflection of it insofar as this creature knows the truth. "For all knowledge of truth is a sort of reflection of and participation in the Eternal Law, which is the unchangeable truth."[13] The Eternal Law is as infinitely distant from written or human law as the divine essence is from created being.

Let us turn now to other senses of the notion of law. I just remarked that the Natural Law is an order based in nature, or required appropriately by human nature, whose regulations are naturally known by man—*naturally*, which is to say, through the inclinations by means of which the rational creature participates in the divine law. The reason that we are concerned with here—since law is an order determined by reason—is that of the author of nature. We do not find this reason in nature itself, as one believed in the XVIIth century. This is why Natural Law obliges *by virtue of* Eternal Law. It is from the divine reason that it possesses its rational character, and consequently, it is from the divine reason that it possesses its genuine nature as law. There would not be any power to oblige, if the reason from which the law emanated was not the divine reason. Other kinds of law oblige only by reason of the eternal law, since it is necessary to have a first source of obligation.

---

[13] [*ST* I-II, 93, 2.]

We can understand at this point in what the error in the conceptions of a thinker like Grotius consisted. While maintaining that Natural Law presupposed in fact God's existence, he wrote the celebrated sentence in which he said that even if, on an absurd supposition, God did not exist, Natural Law would continue to exercise its dominion and its authority over us. The fact is that he was concentrating solely upon the order of nature—as deciphered by human reason—and did not perceive the relationship between the order of nature and the eternal reason.

Two things should be considered here. Suppose, absurdly, that God does not exist and that nothing is changed in things: then, by hypothesis, nature would continue to exist, and consequently the normality of functioning of human nature; the requirements of the ideal order based upon the essence of man would likewise continue to exist. But a second question presents itself: is this order rational, is it wise, does it oblige me in conscience? Indeed, the only foundation for its rationality is the Eternal Law, the divine reason, and it is precisely this which Grotius did not perceive.

Thus began the process (initiated by the scholastic doctors who came after Saint Thomas and who neglected the essential importance of the component knowledge through inclination) of a rationalistic deformation of the concept of Natural Law. At that moment a separation took place, a schism between Eternal Reason and the order of nature. God became merely the guarantor of that order, and Natural Law ceased to be a participation in Eternal Law. It became the order of a nature which was sufficient to herself, an order for which the conceptual and discursive reason provided knowledge. But why should I be obliged in conscience by a purely factual order? In reality, if God does not exist, the Natural Law lacks obligatory power. If the Natural Law does not involve the divine reason, it is not a law, and if it is not a law, it does not oblige.

We should add a few remarks on natural right to the preceding considerations. People sometimes find themselves stuck in inextricable difficulties because they use the terms 'natural right' and 'natural law' (*lex naturalis*) interchangeably, notably because of something that is derived so directly from them that it seems almost to belong to them—I mean (because fortunately there is another word here), the law of civilizations (*jus gentium*).[14] [...]

III. Other Kinds of Law[15]

a. *jus gentium*
With the *jus gentium* (the law of nations),[16] on the contrary, we enter a domain in which the notion of right (*jus*) no longer takes on merely a virtual but a formal and actual meaning as well. For the philosopher or

---

[14] [In current language, these two concepts are expressed in English by the same word, "law." Hence a supplementary difficulty arises. For the sake of clarity, we may be permitted to use the word "right" to signify *jus (droit, Recht),* and the word "law" to signify solely *lex (loi, Gesetz).*]

[15] [From *La loi naturelle* or *loi non écrite,* pp. 51-4; 56-8, 62. Cf. "Natural Law and Moral Law," op. cit. pp. 72-6.]

[16] [We use the expression "law of nations" as equivalent to *jus gentium (le droit des gens),* because the term is so well established in the language of political science and political philosophy, although the term "right of nations" would perhaps correspond better to our use of "positive right" and "natural right." (It is true that the *law* of nations is distinguished in this section from natural and positive *law.*)]

jurist, there is no notion more fraught with difficulties than that of the law of nations. The different theories which have been advanced since the sixteenth century have succeeded in obscuring the concept rather than clarifying it. It is difficult to define the law of nations, because it is intermediary between the Natural Law and the positive law—although Saint Thomas does connect it rather with the positive law. Our thought on the subject would profit greatly if, as a result of the systematic elucidation to which we now proceed, we were able to determine clearly and exactly in what the law of nations consists.

Let us say, then, that in its most profound meaning (as we are able to disengage it from the thought of Saint Thomas), the law of nations—I would prefer to say the common law of civilization—differs from the Natural Law in the manner in which it is known, or in relation to the second essential component, the gnoseological component of the Natural Law. It is necessary to insist on the manner in which the law in question is known. The law of nations is known, not through inclination, but through the conceptual exercise of reason. This is the specific difference distinguishing the law of nations from the Natural Law. The Natural Law is known through inclination, the law of nations is known through the conceptual exercise of the human reason (considered not in such and such an individual, but in common civilized humanity). In this sense, it pertains to the positive law, and for this reason Saint Thomas relates it to positive law: since wherever human reason intervenes as author, we are in the general domain of the positive law. In this case, the human reason does not intervene as the author of the *existence of the law* (which is the case with positive law in the strict sense), but it does intervene as the author of the *knowledge of the law*. In consequence, with the law of nations, we have already a juridical order, no longer virtual as in the case of natural right but formal, although not necessarily written into a code. As to the manner in which the regulations of the law in question are known, it must be said that they are known through the rational, logical, conceptual exercise of the common reason, starting from more profound and more primary principles which are the principles of Natural Law.

Now it is necessary to make a distinction concerning the *content* of the law of nations. In the first place, the law of nations may include regulations pertaining also. to the Natural Law (since the principle of distinction is not the content of the law, but the manner in which the knowledge of the law takes place). Hence, certain regulations which are based upon human nature, and which are connected necessarily with the first principle: "Do good and avoid evil," may be known on the one hand through inclination (in which sense they belong to Natural Law), and on the other hand through the conceptual exercise of reason (in which sense they belong to the law of nations).

Take this example: "We must obey the laws of the social group." This prescription may be a rational conclusion, established through the logical exercise of reason, for the common sense of humanity can deduce it from a more primitive principle: "Men should live in society," in which case we are in the presence of a precept of the law of nations. Now this same regulation: "Obey the laws of the group," is also a norm known not by way of conceptual demonstration, but through inclination, by conformity with the radical tendency which urges men to dwell in society, in which case it is a principle of the Natural Law. Hence the same thing may belong to the Natural Law if it is known through inclination and if the divine reason is the only operative principle causing it to be known as well as to exist, and to the law of nations if it is known by human reason which, intervening between the Divine Reason, the cause of nature, and the knowledge of the precept, acts on its own account and thus introduces an element of positive law.

In the second place, and this is the most general and most interesting case, the content of the law of nations may concern things which, although universally obligatory since they are deduced from a principle of the Natural Law, and although necessarily connected with the first principle: "Do good and avoid evil," go beyond the Natural Law because they are not previously known through inclination but are known *only* as the result of the conceptual exercise of reason, a deduction made not by jurists or philosophers, but by the common reason of humanity. Take this example: "Do not condemn anyone without a hearing." I do not think that this rule is first known through inclination; it is known only as a conclusion logically deduced from what is due in justice to an accused man. In such a case we have a precept of the law of nations which is not a precept of the Natural Law. Similarly, the precept: "Treat prisoners of war humanely," is known only through a logical operation accomplished by the human reason starting from a first principle of the Natural Law.

The law of nations or the common law of civilization has to do with duties which are necessarily bound up with the first principle: "Do good and avoid evil," but in cases like those I have just mentioned, this necessity is seen and established by human reason. And precisely because the regulations dealing with social life are *par excellence* the work of human reason, we have been gradually led to regard the law of nations as pertaining more to the social domain and especially to the international domain. But it is absurd to reduce the law of nations to the laws of international morality.

According to what we have seen, every norm of conduct which is universally valid, but which is known to common consciousness because necessarily deduced by human reason, is a part of jus gentium or the common law of civilization. [...]
The law of nations belongs at once to the moral order and to the juridical order; it presupposes a *debitum morale*, a moral obligation appealing to conscience, before the legal obligation, *debitum legale*. At the same time the law of nations is a formal juridical order, although not necessarily a written one. Hence it differs at once from natural right because it is not merely virtually contained in the order of natural morality, and from positive right because it is not necessarily promulgated by social authority and applied by judiciary authority. It may be formulated juridically; in fact, it seeks to be, but is not necessarily so formulated. Before it is at some future time formulated in the code of a supranational world society whose tribunals would be required to enforce it, the law of nations is first of all formulated in the common conscience by human reason in its legislative role, making the law known through its own conceptual means. In a word, it is based upon the natural order of morality, but it emanates necessarily from this order as the first formal juridical order.

b. **positive law**
We come finally to positive law. The positive law in force in any particular social group, whether it be a question of customary right or written right, has to do with the rights and duties which are bound up in a

contingent, not a necessary, manner with the first principle of the practical intellect: "Do good and avoid evil." And it has as its author not the divine reason but the human reason.[17] By virtue of determined rules of conduct, established by the reason and will of men when they institute the laws or engender the customs of a particular social group, certain things will be good and permissible and certain things bad and not permissible, but it is the human reason which establishes this. Human reason intervenes here as a creative factor not only in that which concerns the knowledge of the law—as in the case of the law of nations—but in that which concerns the very existence of the law. It has the astounding power of laying it down that certain things will henceforth be good and others bad. Thus, for example, a police ordinance has decreed that it will henceforth be good for motorists to stop at the red light and to go when the light is green. There is no kind of natural structure which requires this; it depends uniquely upon the human reason. But once this regulation has been promulgated, it is evil not to stop at the red light. There is thus a moral good and a moral evil which depend upon the human reason because it takes into consideration the particular exigencies of the common good in these given circumstances, in conformity, however, with principles of the Natural Law, as for example: "Do not harm your fellow men." But the Natural Law itself does not prescribe the rules in question, it leaves them to the ultimate determination and initiative of the human reason. The Natural Law

---

[17] [We are speaking here of human positive law and passing over what concerns the divine positive law (which has God for its Author, but whose regulations are contingent with regard to what is required by the nature of the human being).]

itself requires that what it leaves undetermined be ultimately determined by human reason, either concerning necessary things (the *jus gentium*) or concerning contingent matters (the positive law). [...]

Hence, the positive law obliges men in conscience—in other words the *debitum legale* that it institutes is also a *debitum morale*—because it obliges by virtue of the Natural Law. By the same token we see that an unjust law is not a law. This follows as a consequence from what I have just said, that is, from the fact that the positive law obliges by virtue of the Natural Law which is a participation in the Eternal Law. It is inconceivable that an unjust law should oblige by virtue of the Natural Law, by virtue of regulations which go back to the Eternal Law and which are in us a participation in that Law. It is essential to a philosophy such as that of Saint Thomas to regard an unjust law as not obligatory. It is the counterpart of this truth that the just law binds in conscience because it binds by virtue of the Natural Law. If we forget the one, we forget the other.

IV. The Importance of a Rational Foundation for Human Rights[18]

[...] With regard to Human Rights, what matters most to a philosopher is the question of their rational foundations.

The philosophical foundation of the Rights of man is Natural Law. Sorry that we cannot find another word! During the rationalist era jurists and philosophers have misused the notion of natural law to such a degree, either for conservative or for revolutionary purposes,

---

[18] [From *Man and the State* (Chicago: University of Chicago Press, 1951), pp. 80-4.]

they have put it forward in so oversimplified and so
arbitrary a manner, that it is difficult to use it now
without awakening distrust and suspicion in many of
our contemporaries. They should realize, however, that
the history of the rights of man is bound to the history
of Natural Law,[19] and that the discredit into which for
some time positivism brought the idea of Natural Law
inevitably entailed a similar discrediting of the idea of
the Rights of man.

As Mr. Laserson rightly said, "The doctrines of
natural law must not be confused with natural law itself.
The doctrines of natural law, like any other political and
legal doctrines, may propound various arguments or
theories in order to substantiate or justify natural law,
but the overthrow of these theories cannot signify the
overthrow of natural law itself, just as the overthrow of
some theory or philosophy of law does not lead to the
overthrow of law itself. The victory of judicial
positivism in the XIXth Century over the doctrine of
natural law did not signify the death of natural law
itself, but only the victory of the conservative historical
school over the revolutionary rationalistic school, called
for by the general historical conditions in the first half
of the XIXth Century. The best proof of this is the fact
that at the end of that century, the so-called
'renaissance of natural law' was proclaimed."[20]

---

[19] Cf. Heinrich A. Rommen, *Die ewige Wiederkehr des
Naturrrechts* (Leipzig: Hegner, 1936); English trans., *The
Natural Law* (St. Louis: Herder, c1947). See also Charles G.
Haines, *The Revival of Natural Law Concepts* (Cambridge:
Harvard University Press, 1930).

[20] Max M. Laserson, "Positive and 'Natural' Law and their
Correlation," in *Interpretations of Modern Legal Philosophies:
Essays in Honor of Roscoe Pound* [editor Paul Sayre] (New
York: Oxford University Press. 1947), [pp. 434-49].

From the XVIIth Century on, people had begun to think of Nature with a capital N and Reason with a capital R, as abstract divinities sitting in a Platonic heaven. As a result the consonance of a human act with reason was to mean that that act was traced from a ready-made, pre-existing pattern which infallible Reason had been instructed to lay down by infallible Nature, and which, consequently, should be immutably and universally recognized in all places of the earth and at all moments of time. Thus Pascal himself believed that justice among men should of itself have the same universal application as Euclid's propositions. If the human race knew justice, "the brilliance of true equity," he says, "would have subdued all nations, and legislators would not have taken as models, in place of this unchanging justice, the fantasies and caprices of Persians and Germans. One would see it established in all the states of the world and through all the ages. [...]"[21] Which is, I need not say, a wholly abstract and unreal conception of justice. Wait a little more than a century and you will hear Condorcet promulgate this dogma, which at first glance seems self-evident, yet which means nothing: "A good law should be good for everyone"—say, for man of the age of cave-dwellers as well as for man of the age of the steam-engine, for nomadic tribes as well as for agricultural peoples,—"a good law should be good for everyone, just as a true proposition is true for everyone."

So the XVIIIth Century conception of the Rights of man presupposed, no doubt, the long history of the idea of natural law evolved in ancient and mediaeval times;

---

[21] *Pensées*, II, Oeuvres ("Grands écrivains de France," [Paris: Hachette, 1921], Vol. XIII, No. 294), 215.

but it had its immediate origins in the artificial systematization and rationalist recasting to which this idea had been subjected since Grotius and more generally since the advent of a geometrising reason. Through a fatal mistake, natural law—which is *within* the being of things as their very essence is, and which precedes all formulation, and is even known to human reason *not* in terms of conceptual and rational knowledge—natural law was thus conceived after the pattern of a *written* code, applicable to all, of which any just law should be a transcription, and which would determine *a priori* and in all its aspects the norms of human behaviour through ordinances supposedly prescribed by Nature and Reason, but in reality arbitrarily and artificially formulated. "As Warnkoenig has shown, eight or more new systems of natural law made their appearance at every Leipzig booksellers' fair since 1780. Thus Jean Paul Richter's ironical remark contained no exaggeration: Every fair and every war brings forth a new natural law."[22] Moreover, this philosophy of rights ended up, after Rousseau and Kant, by treating the individual as a god and making all the rights ascribed to him the absolute and unlimited rights of a god.

As to God himself, He had only been, from the XVIIth Century on, a superadded guarantor for that trine, self-subsistent absolute: Nature, Reason, Natural Law, which even if God did not exist would still hold sway over men. So that finally the human Will or human Freedom, also raised to Platonic self-subsistence in that intelligible, though unreachable, empyreal world which Kant inherited from Leibniz, was to replace God in actual fact as supreme source and origin of Natural

---

[22] Rommen, op. cit., p. 106.

Law. Natural Law was to be deduced from the so-called autonomy of the Will (there is a genuine notion of autonomy, that of Saint Paul—unfortunately the XVIIIth Century had forgotten it). The rights of the human person were to be based on the claim that man is subject to no law other than that of his own will and freedom. "A person," Kant wrote, "is subject to no other laws than those which he (either alone or jointly with others) gives to himself."[23] In other words, man must "obey only himself," as Jean-Jacques Rousseau put it,[24] because every measure or regulation springing from the world of nature (and finally from creative wisdom) would destroy at one and the same time his autonomy and his supreme dignity.

This philosophy built no solid foundations for the rights of the human person, because nothing can be founded on illusion: it compromised and squandered these rights, because it led men to conceive them as rights in themselves divine, hence infinite, escaping every objective measure, denying every limitation imposed upon the claims of the ego, and ultimately expressing the absolute independence of the human subject and a so-called absolute right — which

---

[23] *Introduction to the Metaphysics of Morals*, IV, 24. [Akademie ed., 223] [See Immanuel Kant, *The Metaphysics of Morals*, tr. Mary Gregor (Cambridge: Cambridge University Press, 1991) p. 50.]

[24] ["'The problem is to find a form of association which will defend and protect with the whole common force the person and goods of each associate, and in which each, while uniting himself with all, may still obey himself alone, and remain as free as before.' This is the fundamental problem of which the Social Contract provides the solution." Jean-Jacques Rousseau, *The Social Contract*, Book I. Ch. 6 (tr. G. D. H. Cole, London: J.M. Dent, 1913). Ed.]

supposedly pertains to everything in the human subject by the mere fact that it is in him—to unfold one's cherished possibilities at the expense of all other beings. When men thus instructed clashed on all sides with the impossible, they came to believe in the bankruptcy of the rights of the human person. Some have turned against these rights with an enslaver's fury; some have continued to invoke them, while in their inmost conscience they are weighed down by a temptation to scepticism which is one of the most alarming symptoms of the crisis of our civilization

V. Natural Law and Human Rights[25]

I need not apologize for having dwelt so long on the subject of natural law. How could we understand human rights if we had not a sufficiently adequate notion of natural law? The same natural law which lays down our most fundamental duties, and by virtue of which every law is binding, is the very law which assigns to us our fundamental rights.[26] It is because we are enmeshed in

---

[25] [From *Man and the State* (Chicago: University of Chicago Press, 1951), pp. 95-7 This follows very closely Maritain's exposition in *The Rights of Man and the Natural Law* (New York: Scribner's, 1943), pp. 66-9.]

[26] Cf. Edward S. Dore, associate justice of New York Supreme Court, "Human Rights and Natural Law," *New York Law Journal,* 1946; [Harold R.] McKinnon, "The Higher Law [: Reaction has Permeated our Legal Thinking]," *American Bar Association Journal,* [Vol. 33]: [February] 1947 [pp. 106-9; 202-4]; Laserson, *op. cit.;* Lord [Robert Alderson] Wright, chairman of the United Nations War Crimes Commission, "Natural Law and International Law," [*Interpretations of Modern Legal Philosophies:*] *Essays in Honor of Roscoe Pound,* op. cit., pp. 794-807; Godfrey P. Schmidt, "An Approach to the Natural Law" [*Fordham Law Review,* Vol.

the universal order, in the laws and regulations of the cosmos and of the immense family of created natures (and finally in the order of creative wisdom), and it is because we have at the same time the privilege of sharing in spiritual nature, that we possess rights vis-à-vis other men and all the assemblage of creatures.[27] In

---

XIX, No. 1, March 1950, pp 1-42.]
The concept of Natural Law played, as is well known. a basic part in the thought of the Founding Fathers. In insisting (cf. Cornelia Geer Le Boutillier, *American Democracy and Natural Law* [New York: Columbia University Press, 1950], chap. iii) that they were men of government rather than metaphysicians and that they used the concept for practical rather than philosophical purpose, in a more or less vague, even in a "utilitarianist," sense (as if any concern for the common good and the implementing of the ends of human life were to be labeled utilitarianism), one makes only more manifest the impossibility of tearing Natural Law away from the moral tenets upon which this country was founded.

In his vigorous and stimulating book, *Courts on Trial* (Princeton, NJ: Princeton University Press, 1949), Judge Jerome Frank also views Natural Law more in a practical than in a metaphysical perspective. This very fact gives a particularly significant experiential value to his judgment, when he writes: "No decent non-Catholic can fail to accept the few basic Natural Law principles or precepts as representing, at the present time and for any reasonably foreseeable future, essential parts of the foundation of civilization" (pp. 364-5).

Be it finally noted that when it comes to the application of basic requirements of justice in cases where positive law's provisions are lacking to a certain extent, a recourse to the principles of Natural Law is unavoidable, thus creating a precedent and new judicial rules. That is what happened, in a remarkable manner, with the epoch-making Nazi war crimes trial in Nuremberg.

[27] [In Maritain's papers, conserved at Kolbheim, there is a manuscript of an essay entitled "The Philosophical Foundations of Natural Law." There is no indication of whether this essay

the last analysis, as every creature acts by virtue of its
Principle, which is the Pure Act; as every authority
worthy of the name (that is to say, just) is binding in
conscience by virtue of the Principle of beings, which is
pure Wisdom: so too every right possessed by man is
possessed by virtue of the right possessed by God, Who
is pure Justice, to see the order of His wisdom in beings
respected, obeyed, and loved by every intelligence. It is
essential to law to be an order of *reason;* and natural
law, or the normality of functioning of human nature
known by knowledge through inclination, is *law*,
binding in conscience, only because nature and the
inclinations of nature manifest an order of reason,—that
is of *Divine Reason*. Natural law is law only because it
is a participation in Eternal Law.

At this point we see that a positivistic philosophy
recognizing Fact alone—as well as either an idealistic

---

was ever delivered as a lecture or published. It is almost
identical to *Man and the State*, Chapter IV, though some of the
material is rearranged and the essay adds a small amount of
new material. Maritain provides the following important
definition of 'right'—a definition which does not appear in his
other texts:

> What does the notion of right mean? A right is a
> requirement that emanates from a self with regard to
> something which is understood as *his* due, and of which
> the other moral agents are obliged in conscience not to
> deprive him. The normality of functioning of the
> creature endowed with intellect and free will implies
> the fact that this creature has duties and obligations; it
> also implies the fact that this creature possesses rights,
> by virtue of his very nature—because he is a self with
> whom the other selves are confronted, and whom they
> are not free to deprive of what is due him. And the
> normality of functioning of the rational creature is an
> expression of the order of divine wisdom.]

or a materialistic philosophy of absolute Immanence—is powerless to establish the existence of rights which are naturally possessed by the human being, prior and superior to written legislation and to agreements between governments, rights which the civil society does not have to *grant* but to *recognize* and sanction as universally valid, and which no social necessity can authorize us even momentarily to abolish or disregard. Logically, the concept of such rights can seem only a superstition to these philosophies. It is only valid and rationally tenable if each existing individual has a nature or essence which is the locus of intelligible necessities and necessary truths, that is to say, if the realm of Nature taken as a constellation of facts and events envelops and reveals a realm of Nature taken as a universe of Essences transcending the fact and the event. In other words there is no right unless a certain order—which can be violated in fact—is inviolably required by *what things are* in their intelligible type or their essence, or by what the nature of man is, and is cut out for: an order by virtue of which certain things like life, work, freedom are due to the human person, an existent who is endowed with a spiritual soul and free will. Such an order, which is not a factual datum in things, but demands to be realized by them, and which imposes itself upon our minds to the point of binding us in conscience, exists in things in a certain way, I mean as a requirement of their essence. But that very fact, the fact that things participate in an ideal order which transcends their existence and requires to govern it, would not be possible if the foundation of this ideal order, like the foundation of essences themselves and eternal truths, did not exist in a separate Spirit, in an Absolute which is superior to the world, in what perennial philosophy calls the Eternal Law.

For a philosophy which recognizes Fact alone, the notion of Value,—I mean Value objectively true in itself—is not conceivable. How, then, can one claim rights if one does not believe in values? If the affirmation of the intrinsic value and dignity of man is nonsense, the affirmation of the natural rights of man is nonsense also.

VI. Law in General and Human Rights[28]

Let us now discuss further some problems which deal with human rights in general.

a. The different kinds of law and human rights[29]
My first point will relate to the distinction between Natural Law and Positive Law. One of the main errors of the rationalist philosophy of human rights has been to regard positive law as a mere transcript traced off from natural law, which would supposedly prescribe in the name of Nature all that which positive law prescribes in the name of society. They forgot the immense field of human things which depend on the variable conditions of social life and on the free initiative of human reason, and which natural law leaves undetermined.

As I have pointed out, *natural law* deals with the rights and the duties which are connected in a *necessary* manner with the first principle: "Do good and avoid evil." This is why the precepts of the unwritten law are in themselves or in the nature of things (I am not saying in man's knowledge of them) universal and invariable.

---

[28] [From *Man and the State*, op. cit., pp. 97-107.]

[29] [This section follows very closely Maritain's presentation in *The Rights of Man and Natural Law*, pp. 69-73.]

Jus gentium, or the *Law of Nations,* is difficult to define exactly, because it is intermediary between natural law and positive law. Let us say that in its deepest and most genuine meaning, such as put forward by Thomas Aquinas, the law of nations, or better to say, the common law of civilization, differs from natural law because it is *known,* not through inclination, but through the *conceptual exercise of reason,* or through rational knowledge;[30] in this sense it pertains to positive law,

---

[30] According to Saint Thomas *(ST* I-II, 95. 4), *jus gentium*—which he sharply distinguishes from natural law and connects rather with positive law—is concerned with all things that derive from natural law as *conclusions* from principles.

Yet he also teaches that the *propria principia* of Natural Law are like conclusions derived from *principia communia (ST* I-II, 94. 4, 5, and 6). And assuredly the *propria principia* of natural law belong to Natural Law, not to *jus gentium!* Well, in *ST* 95. 2, Saint Thomas gives the prohibition of murder as an example of a conclusion derived from a principle of natural law ("do nobody evil"), and pertaining to what is defined as *jus gentium* in art. 4. It is obvious, however, that the prohibition of murder, which is inscribed in the Decalogue, is a precept of natural law. What then?

The only way to realize the inner consistency of all that, and correctly to grasp the Thomistic distinction between Natural Law and *jus gentium,* is to understand that a precept which is *like a* conclusion derived from a principle of natural law but which in actual fact is *known through inclination, not through rational deduction, is* part of *natural law;* but that a precept which is *known through rational deduction, and as a conclusion conceptually inferred* from a principle of natural law, is part of *jus gentium.* The latter pertains to positive law more than to natural law precisely by virtue of the manner in which it is known and because of the intervention of human reason in the establishment of the precepts conceptually concluded (whereas the *only* reason on which natural law depends is divine Reason). The prohibition of murder, in so far as this precept is *known by inclination,* belongs to natural law. The same prohibition of

and formally constitutes a juridical order (though not necessarily written in a code).

But as concerns its content, *jus gentium* comprises both things which belong also to natural law (insofar as they are not only known as rationally inferred, but also known through inclination) and things which—though obligatory in a universal manner, since concluded from a principle of natural law—are beyond the content of natural law (because they are *only* rationally inferred, and not known through inclination). In both cases *jus gentium* or the common law of civilization deals, like natural law, with rights and duties which are connected with the first principle in a *necessary* manner. And precisely because it is known through rational knowledge, and is itself a work of reason, it is more especially concerned with such rights and duties as exist in the realm of the basic natural work achieved by human reason, that is, the state of civil life.

Positive Law, or the body of laws (either customary law or statute law) in force in a given social group, deals with the rights and the duties which are connected with the first principle, but in a *contingent* manner, by virtue of the determinate ways of conduct set down by the reason and the will of man when they institute the laws or give birth to the customs of a particular society, thus stating of themselves that in the particular group in question certain things will be good and permissible, certain other things bad and not permissible.

But it is by virtue of natural law that the law of Nations and positive law take on the force of law, and impose themselves upon the conscience. They are a prolongation or an extension of natural law, passing into

---

murder, if this precept is known as a conclusion *rationally* inferred from a principle of natural law, pertains to *jus gentium.*

objective zones which can less and less be sufficiently determined by the essential inclinations of human nature. For it is *natural law itself which requires that whatever it leaves undetermined shall subsequently be determined*, either as a right or a duty existing for all men, and of which they are made aware, not by knowledge through inclination, but by conceptual reason—that's for *jus gentium* or—this is for positive law—as a right or a duty existing for certain men by reason of the human and contingent regulations proper to the social group of which they are a part. Thus there are imperceptible transitions (at least from the point of view of historical experience) between Natural Law, the Law of Nations, and Positive Law. There is a dynamism which impels the unwritten law to flower forth in human law, and to render the latter ever more perfect and just in the very field of its contingent determinations. It is in accordance with this dynamism that the rights of the human person take political and social form in the community.

Man's right to existence, to personal freedom, and to the pursuit of the perfection of moral life, belongs, strictly speaking, to natural law.

The right to the private ownership of material goods[31] pertains to natural law, insofar as mankind is

---

[31] Cf. my work, *Freedom in the Modern World* (New York: Charles Scribner's Sons, 1936), Appendix I.

[The right to the private ownership of material goods relates to the human person as an extension of the person itself, for, enmeshed in matter and without natural protection for its existence and its freedom, it must have the power to acquire and possess in order to make up for the protection which nature does not afford it. On the other hand, the use of private property must always be such as to serve the common good, in one fashion or

naturally entitled to possess for its own common use the material goods of nature; it pertains to the law of Nations, or *jus gentium*, in so far as reason necessarily concludes that for the sake of the common good those material goods must be privately owned, as a result of the conditions naturally required for their management and for human work (I mean human work performed in a genuinely human manner, ensuring the freedom of the human person in the face of the community). And the particular modalities of the right to private ownership, which vary according to the form of a society and the state of the development of its economy, are determined by positive law.

The freedom of nations to live unburdened by the yoke of want or distress ("freedom from want") and the freedom for them to live unburdened by the yoke of fear or terror ("freedom from fear"), as President Roosevelt defined them in his Four Points[32], correspond to

---

another, and to be advantageous to all, for in the first place it is to Man, to the human species generally, that material goods are granted by nature. (From *The Rights of Man and Natural Law*, pp. 71-2, note 1)]

[32] ["(1) Freedom of speech and expression everywhere in the world. (2) Freedom of every person to worship God in his own way everywhere in the world. (3) Freedom from want which, translated into world terms, means economic understanding which will secure to every nation a healthy peace-time life for its inhabitants everywhere in the world. (4) Freedom from fear which, translated into world terms, means a world-wide reduction of armaments to such a point and in such a thorough fashion that no nation will be in a position to commit an act of aggression against any neighbor anywhere." (These "four essential human freedoms" were articulated by President Franklin D. Roosevelt in his Annual Message to the United States Congress, on January 6, 1941.) Cf. Maritain's *The Rights of Man and Natural Law*, p. 72, note 1.]

requirements of the law of Nations which are to be
fulfilled by positive law and by a possible economic and
political organization of the civilized world.

The right of suffrage granted to each one of us for
the election of the officials of the State arises from
positive law, determining the way in which the natural
right of the people to self-government has to apply in a
democratic society.

b. The alienability of human rights

My second point will deal with the inalienable character
of natural human rights. They are inalienable since they
are grounded on the very nature of man, which of
course no man can lose. This does not mean that they
reject by nature any limitation, or that they are the
infinite rights of God. Just as every law,—notably the
natural law, on which they are grounded,—aims at the
common good, so human rights have an intrinsic
relation to the common good. Some of them, like the
right to existence or to the pursuit of happiness, are of
such a nature that the common good would be
jeopardized if the body politic could restrict in any
measure the possession that men naturally have of them.
Let us say that they are absolutely inalienable. Others,
like the right of association or of free speech, are of
such a nature that the common good would be
jeopardized if the body politic could not restrict in some
measure (all the less as societies are more capable of
and based upon common freedom) the possession that
men naturally have of them. Let us say that they are
inalienable only substantially.

* * *

Yet, even absolutely inalienable rights are liable to
limitation, if not as to their possession, at least as to

their exercise. So my third point will deal with the distinction between the *possession* and the *exercise* of a right. Even for the absolutely inalienable rights, we must distinguish between possession and exercise—the latter being subject to conditions and limitations dictated in each case by justice. If a criminal can be justly condemned to die, it is because by his crime he has deprived himself, let us not say of the right to live, but of the possibility of justly asserting this right: he has morally cut himself off from the human community, precisely as regards the use of this fundamental and "inalienable" right which the punishment inflicted upon him prevents him from exercising.

The right to receive the heritage of human culture through education is also a fundamental, absolutely inalienable right: the exercise of it is subject to a given society's concrete possibilities; and it can be contrary to justice to claim the use of this right for each and all *hic et nunc* if that can only be realized by ruining the social body, as in the case of the slave society of ancient Rome or the feudal society of the Middle Ages—though of course this claim to education for all remained legitimate, as something to be fulfilled in time. In such cases what remains is to endeavor to change the social state involved. We see from this example—and I note this parenthetically—that the basis for the secret stimulus which incessantly fosters the transformation of societies lies in the fact that man possesses inalienable rights but is deprived of the possibility of justly claiming the *exercise* of certain of these rights because of the inhuman element that remains in the social structure of each period.

This distinction between the possession and the exercise of a right is, in my opinion, of serious importance. I have just indicated how it enables us to explain the limitations that can be justly imposed upon the assertion of certain rights under certain circumstances, either by the guilt of some delinquent or criminal individual, or by social structures whose vice or primitiveness prevents the claim, legitimate in itself, from being immediately fulfilled without encroaching upon major rights.

I should like to add that this distinction also enables us to understand that it is fitting at times, as history advances, to forego the exercise of certain rights which we nevertheless continue to possess. These considerations apply to many problems concerning either the modalities of private property in a society that is in the process of economic transformation, or the limitations on the so-called "sovereignty" of States in an international community that is in the process of being organized.

c. **Human rights in particular**
Coming finally to the problems dealing with the enumeration of human rights taken in particular, I shall first recall to our minds what I have previously stated: namely the fact that in natural law there is immutability as regards things, or the law itself ontologically considered, but progress and relativity as regards human awareness of it. We have especially a tendency to inflate and make absolute, limitless, unrestricted in every respect, the rights of which we are aware, thus blinding ourselves to any other right which would counterbalance them. Thus in human history no "new" right, I mean no right of which common consciousness was becoming newly aware, has been recognized in actual fact without having had to struggle against and overcome the bitter opposition of some "old rights." That was the story of the right to a just wage and similar

rights in the face of the right to free mutual agreement and the right to private ownership. The fight of the latter to claim for itself a privilege of divine, limitless absolutism was the unhappy epic of the XIXth Century. (Another unhappy epic was to follow, in which on the contrary the very principle of private ownership was under fire, and every other personal freedom with it.) Well! In 1850, when the law against fugitive slaves was enforced, was not any help given to a fugitive slave held by the conscience of many people to be a criminal attempt against the right to ownership?

Conversely "new" rights often wage war against the "old" ones, and cause them to be unfairly disregarded. At the time of the French Revolution, for instance, a law promulgated in 1791 prohibited as "an attack on freedom and on the Declaration of the Rights of Man" any attempt by workers to associate in trade unions and join forces in refusing to work except for a given wage. This was considered an indirect return to the old system of corporations.

As concerns the problems of the present time, it is obvious that human reason has now become aware not only of the rights of man as a human and a civic person, but also of his rights as a social person engaged in the process of production and consumption, especially of his rights as a working person.

Generally speaking, a new age of civilization will be called upon to recognize and define the rights of the human being in his social, economic, and cultural functions—producers' and consumers' rights, technicians' rights, rights of those who devote themselves to labor of the mind, rights of everyone to share in the educational and cultural heritage of civilized life. But the most urgent problems are concerned on the one hand with the rights of that

primordial society which is family society, and which is prior to the political state; on the other hand with the rights of the human being as he is engaged in the function of labor.[33]
I am alluding to rights such as the right to work and freely to choose one's work.—The right freely to form vocational groups or unions.—The right of the worker to be considered socially as an adult, and to have, some way or other, a share and active participation in the responsibilities of economic life.—The right of economic groups (unions and working communities) and other social groups to freedom and autonomy.—The right to a just wage, that is, sufficient to secure the family's living.—The right to relief, unemployment insurance, sick benefits, and social security.—The right to have a part, free of charge, depending on the possibilities of the social body, in the elementary goods, both material and spiritual, of civilization.

What is involved in all this is first of all the dignity of work, the feeling for the rights of the human person in the worker, the rights in the name of which the worker stands before his employer in a relationship of justice and as an adult person, not as a child or as a servant. There is here an essential datum which far surpasses every problem of merely economic and social technique, for it is a *moral* datum, affecting man in his spiritual depths.

I am convinced that the antagonism between the "old" and the "new" rights of man—I mean the social

---

[33] Cf. our book, *The Rights of Man and Natural Law* (New York: Charles Scribner's Sons, 1943); Georges Gurvitch, *La Déclaration des droits sociaux* (New York: Maison Française. 1944) [English translation: *The Bill of Social Rights* (New York: International Universities Press, 1946)].

rights to which I just alluded, especially those which relate to social justice and aim both at the efficacy of the social group and at the freedom from want and economic bondage of the working person—I am convinced that that antagonism, which many contemporary writers take pleasure in magnifying, is by no means insuperable. These two categories of rights seem irreconcilable only because of the clash between the two opposed ideologies and political systems which appeal to them, and of which they are independent in actual reality. Too much stress cannot be placed on the fact that the recognition of a particular category of rights is not the privilege of one school of thought at the expense of the others; it is no more necessary to be a follower of Rousseau to recognize the rights of the individual than it is to be a Marxist to recognize the economic and social rights. As a matter of fact, the universal Declaration of the Rights of Man adopted and proclaimed by the United Nations on December 10, 1948, makes room for the "old" and the "new" rights together.[34]

If each of the human rights were by its nature absolutely unconditional and exclusive of any limitation, like a divine attribute, obviously any conflict between them would be irreconcilable. But who does not know in reality that these rights, being human, are, like everything human, subject to conditioning and limitation, at least, as we have seen, as far as their exercise is concerned? That the various rights ascribed

---

[34] Even after the first World War, the Declarations of Rights attached to the new constitutions which then appeared on the European scene recognized the importance of social rights. Cf. Boris Mirkine-Guetzevitch, *Les nouvelles tendances du droit constitutionnel* (Paris: Giard, 1931), chap. iii.

to the human being limit each other, particularly that the economic and social rights, the rights of man as a person involved in the life of the community, cannot be given room in human history without restricting, to some extent, the freedoms and rights of man as an individual person, is only normal. What creates irreducible differences and antagonisms among men is the determination of the degree of such restriction, and more generally the determination of the scale of values that governs the exercise and the concrete organization of these various rights. Here we are confronted with the clash between incompatible political philosophies. Because here we are no longer dealing with the simple recognition of the diverse categories of human rights, but with the principle of dynamic unification in accordance with which they are carried into effect; we are dealing with the tonality, the specific key, by virtue of which different music is played on this same keyboard, either in harmony or in discord with human dignity.

We can imagine—in accordance with the views set forward in the first part of this chapter—that the advocates of a liberal-individualistic, a communistic, or a personalist[35] type of society will lay down on paper similar, perhaps identical, lists of the rights of man. They will not, however, play that instrument in the same way. Everything depends upon the supreme value in accordance with which all these rights will be ordered and will mutually limit each other. It is by virtue of the hierarchy of values to which we thus subscribe that we

---

[35] Cf. our books, *Freedom in the Modern World*, pp. 46 ff., and *True Humanism* (New York: Charles Scribner's Sons, 1938), pp. 127 ff. [Cf. the later, improved, translation, *Integral Humanism*, tr. Joseph Evans (New York: Scribners, 1968), pp. 133 ff.]

determine the way in which the rights of man, economic and social as well as individual, should, in our eyes, pass into the realm of existence. Those whom, for want of a better name, I just called the advocates of a liberal-individualistic type of society, see the mark of human dignity first and foremost in the power of each person to appropriate individually the goods of nature in order to do freely whatever he wants; the advocates of a communistic type of society see the mark of human dignity first and foremost in the power to submit these same goods to the collective command of the social body in order to "free" human labor (by subduing it to the economic community) and to gain the control of history; the advocates of a personalistic type of society see the mark of human dignity first and foremost in the power to make these same goods of nature serve the common conquest of intrinsically human, moral, and spiritual goods and of man's freedom of autonomy. Those three groups inevitably will accuse each other of ignoring certain essential rights of the human being. It remains to be seen who makes a faithful image and who a distorted image of man. As far as I am concerned, I know where I stand: with the third of the three schools of thought I just mentioned.

Chapter 4

Natural Rights[36]

In this Chapter, Maritain extends his account of natural right. Not only do we learn more of what Maritain considers 'natural right' to involve, but we become aware again of the historical— though not historicist—character of such rights. Many of these rights appear in the United Nations Declaration of 1948, but there they appear without any argument; here Maritain provides some of the background necessary for a complete theory of natural rights. While Maritain distinguishes 'the rights of the human person' from 'the rights of the civic person' and 'the rights of the working person,' it would be a mistake to assume that only the first group are natural rights.

I. The Rights of the Human Person

The universe of truths—of science, of wisdom and of poetry—towards which the intelligence tends by itself, belongs, by nature, to a plane higher than the political community. The power of the State and of social interests cannot impose itself upon this universe. (Although it can and must oppose, within the social body, the propagation of errors which might threaten the fundamental ethics of common life and the principles on which it is founded.)[37] [...] [T]he

---

[36] [From *The Rights of Man and Natural Law* (New York: Scribner's, 1943), pp. 76-99; 102-114.]

[37] Cf. Yves Simon, "Liberty and Authority," in *Proceedings of the American Catholic Philosophical Association*, Vol. XVI (1940) [*The Problem of Liberty*, ed. Charles A. Hart.

State can, under certain definite circumstances, ask a mathematician to teach mathematics, a philosopher to teach philosophy—these are functions of the social body. But the State cannot force a philosopher or a mathematician to adopt a philosophical doctrine or a mathematical doctrine, for these things depend solely and exclusively upon truth.

The secret of the heart and the free act as such, the universe of moral laws, the right of conscience to hearken unto God, and to make its way to Him—all these things, in the natural as in the supernatural order, cannot be tampered with by the State nor fall into its clutches. Doubtless law binds in conscience, yet this is because it is law only if just and promulgated by legitimate authority, not because the majority or the State can be the standard of conscience. Doubtless, the State has a moral and not merely material function; the law has an educational function and tends to develop moral virtues; the State has the right to punish me if, my conscience being blind, I follow my conscience and commit an act in itself criminal or unlawful. But in like circumstances the State has not the authority to make me reform the judgment of my conscience, any more than it has the power of imposing upon intellects its own judgment of good and evil, or of legislating on divine matters, or of imposing any religious faith whatsoever. The State knows this well. And that is why, whenever it goes beyond its natural limits, in the name of some totalitarian pretension, and enters into the sanctuary of the conscience, it strives to violate this sanctuary by monstrous means of psychological poisoning, organized lies and terror.

(Washington, DC: Catholic University of America, 1940)] pp. 86-114.

Every human person has the right to make its own decisions with regard to its personal destiny, whether it be a question of choosing one's work, of marrying the man or woman of one's choice or of pursuing a religious vocation. In the case of extreme peril and for the safety of the community, the State can forcibly requisition the services of each of us and demand that each risk his life in a just war; it can also deprive criminals of certain of their rights (or rather sanction the fact that they themselves forfeited them); for example, men judged unworthy of exercising parental authority. But the State becomes iniquitous and tyrannical if it claims to base the functioning of civil life on forced labour, or if it tries to violate the rights of the family in order to become master of men's souls. For just as man is constituted a person, made for God and for a life superior to time, before being constituted a part of the political community, so too man is constituted a part of family society before being constituted a part of political society. The end for which the family exists is to produce and bring up human persons and prepare them to fulfil their total destiny. And if the State too has an educative function, if education is not outside its sphere, this function is to help the family fulfil its mission, and to complement this mission, not to efface in the child his vocation as a human person and replace it by that of a living tool and material for the State.

To sum up, the fundamental rights, like the right to existence and life; the right to personal freedom or to conduct one's own life as master of oneself and of one's acts, responsible for them before God and the law of the community; the right to the pursuit of the perfection of

moral and rational human life;[38] the right to the pursuit
of eternal good (without this pursuit there is no true
pursuit of happiness); the right to keep one's body
whole; the right to private ownership of material goods,
which is a safeguard of the liberties of the individual;
the right to marry according to one's choice and to raise
a family which will be assured of the liberties due it;
the right of association, the respect for human dignity in
each individual, whether or not he represents an
economic value for society—all these rights are rooted
in the vocation of the person (a spiritual and free agent)
to the order of absolute values and to a destiny superior
to time. The French Declaration of the Rights of Man
framed these rights in the altogether rationalist point of
view of the Enlightenment and the Encyclopedists, and
to that extent enveloped them in ambiguity. The
American Declaration of Independence, however
marked by the influence of Locke and "natural
religion," adhered more closely to the originally
Christian character of human rights.

The rationalism of the Encyclopedists, making of
natural law no longer an offspring of creative wisdom
but a revelation of reason unto itself, transformed
natural law into a code of absolute and universal justice
inscribed in nature and deciphered by reason as an
ensemble of geometric theorems or speculative data;
and into this code of nature this same rationalism
absorbed every kind of law which became thenceforth
as necessary and universal as nature itself. It is

---

[38] In this above all consists the pursuit of happiness: the pursuit
of happiness here on earth is the pursuit, not of material
advantages, but of moral righteousness, of the strength and
perfection of the soul, with the material and social conditions
thereby implied.

doubtless because of this false rationalist perspective, but it is also because of the corruption of Christian principles within the social and political life of the ancient regime, that the affirmation of rights themselves based on Christian principles appeared revolutionary with regard to the Christian tradition. "To the Pilgrim Fathers, making their constitutions in New England in the seventeenth century, these Rights had a Christian origin."[39] The consciousness of the rights of the person really has its origin in the conception of man and of natural law established by centuries of Christian philosophy.

The first of these rights is that of the human person to make its way towards its eternal destiny along the path which its conscience has recognized as the path indicated by God. *With respect to God and truth*, one has not the right to choose according to his own whim any path whatsoever, he must choose the true path, in so far as it is in his power to know it. But *with respect to the State, to the temporal community and to the temporal power*, he is free to choose his religious path at his own risk,[40] his freedom of conscience is a natural, inviolable right.[41]

---

[39] The Bishop of Chichester [George Kennedy Allen Bell], *Christianity and World Order*, ([Harmondsworth:] Penguin Books, 1940), p. 104.

[40] If this religious path goes so very far afield that it leads to acts repugnant to natural law and the security of the State, the latter has the right to interdict and apply sanctions against these acts. This does not mean that it has authority in the realm of conscience.

[41] This is how we must understand the right which President [Franklin D.] Roosevelt describes as the "freedom of every person to worship God in his own way everywhere in the world."

I have just spoken of the right of the human person to raise a family and the rights of the family community itself. Here the person is no longer considered merely as an individual person. It is by virtue of the fact that it is part of a group that special rights are accorded at the same time to it and to the group in question. The rights of the family, the rights of the human person as father or mother of the family, belong to natural law in the strictest sense of the word.

The same must be said of the rights and liberties of spiritual and religious families, which are at the same time the rights and liberties of the person in the spiritual and religious order. These rights and liberties belong to natural law—not to mention the superior right which the Church invokes by reason of her divine foundation.

II. The Rights of the Civic Person

But when you come to the rights of the civic person, in other words political rights, these spring directly from positive law and from the fundamental constitution of the political community. And they depend indirectly upon natural law, not merely because in a general manner the regulations of human law fulfil an aim of natural law by completing that which natural law leaves undetermined, but also because the manner in which this completion takes place corresponds, in the case of political rights, to an aspiration inscribed in man's nature. Here we find ourselves confronted with the dynamism of which I spoke a moment ago, by virtue of which positive law tends to express in its own sphere requirements which, on a deeper level, are those of natural law itself, in such fashion that these requirements expand more and more into the very sphere of human law. It is by reason of a more perfect agreement with the fundamental demands of natural law that human law passes on to higher degrees of justice and perfection.

The famous saying of Aristotle that man is a political animal does not mean only that man is naturally made to live in society; it also means that man naturally asks to lead a political life and to participate actively in the life of the political community. It is upon this postulate of human nature that political liberties and political rights rest, and particularly the right of suffrage. Perhaps it is easier for men to renounce active participation in political life; in certain cases it may even have happened that they felt happier and freer from care while dwelling in the commonwealth as political slaves; or while passively handing over to their leaders all the care of the management of the community. But in this case they gave up a privilege proper to their nature, one of these privileges which, in a sense, make life more difficult and which bring with them a greater or lesser amount of labour, strain and suffering, but which correspond to human dignity. A state of civilization in which men, as individual persons, by a free choice designate those who shall hold authority, is in itself a more perfect state. For if it is true that political authority has as its essential function the direction of free men towards the common good, it is normal for these free men to choose by themselves those who have the function of leading them: this is the most elementary form of active participation in political life. That is why universal suffrage, by means of which every adult human person has, as such, the right to make his opinion felt regarding the affairs of the community by casting his vote in the election of the people's representatives and the officers of the State— that is why universal suffrage has a wholly fundamental political and human value and is one of those rights which a community of free men can never give up.

Thus we see that because of the very fact that every person as such should normally be able to make his thought and his will felt in political matters, it is also normal for the members of political society to group themselves, according to the affinity of their ideas and aspirations, into political parties of political schools. Much has been said against political parties, and these reproaches are justified by all the abuses which have corrupted their functioning, and which have paralysed and caused the degeneration of the European democracies. These vices, however, are not essential to the very notion of these groups, whose diversity corresponds to the natural diversity of practical conceptions and perspectives existing among the members of the political community. Moreover, it has justly been pointed out[42] that the Single Party system established in the totalitarian states, far from remedying them, brings to a peak the vices and the tyranny with which the adversaries of democracy reproach the party system. The totalitarian Single Party system is the worst form and the catastrophe of the party system. What we ask of a new Democracy is not to abolish political parties, but rather to regulate the make-up of the State, of the legislative assemblies and the organs of government, in such a manner that the latter, while subject to the control of the assemblies in matters of major interest, would be freed from party domination.

---

[42] Cf. Yves Simon, "Thomism and Democracy," [in *Science, Philosophy and Religion: Second Symposium*, eds. Louis Finkelstein and Lyman Bryson (New York: The Conference on Science, Philosophy and Religion in their Relations to the Democratic Way of Life, Inc. 1942), pp. 258-72.]

This problem is not like that of squaring the circle, and such a recasting is perfectly conceivable in a new Democracy.

I have stressed first of all the rights of the civic person, of the human individual as a citizen. Therein lies the root of a true political democracy. On the other hand, as I remarked just above on the subject of the family, when the person is considered as part of a group, the rights which are acknowledged to him are also, and at the same stroke, the rights of the group in question. Here the rights of the civic person are the same thing as the rights of the people. The right of the people to take unto itself the constitution and the form of government of its choice is the first and most fundamental of political rights. Such a right is subject only to the requirements of justice and natural law. Moreover, in order for these rights of the people to be firmly secured, the constitutional form of the political State is a prime necessity. All civilized peoples have had a fundamental constitution, but, in the past, it was often more a matter of consent and tradition than of juridical institution. A constitution juridically formulated and established, by virtue of the will of the people deciding freely to live under the political forms thus set up, corresponds to an achieved progress in the grasp of political consciousness and in political organization; here is a characteristic feature of every true democracy. The constitution established by the people is the right of the people, as the rights and liberties of the citizen are the right of the civic person.

There are other rights of the civic person, in particular those summed up by the three equalities: political equality assuring to each citizen his status, security and liberties within the State; equality of all before the law, implying an independent judiciary

power which assures to each one the right to call upon
the law and to be restrained by it alone if it has been
violated; equal admission of all citizens to public
employment according to their capacity, and free access
of all to the various professions, without racial or social
discrimination. Let us note in this connection that the
prerogatives enjoyed by the citizens of a country
generally relate to their strictly political status and to
their participation (through the right to vote, for
instance) in the administration of the State. As for the
rest, the rights of the civic person are the privilege of
every man, citizen or foreigner, who, by his residence in
a country which respects the Law of Nations, is called
upon to share in civilized life.[43]

In all the preceding analyses I have limited myself
to essentials. I should like merely to propose two more
observations concerning the right of association and
freedom of expression.

The right of association is a natural right which
takes political form when it is sanctioned by the State
and subject to the regulations of the State concerning
the common good (the State has the right to prohibit and
dissolve—not arbitrarily, but according to the decision
of appropriate juridical institutions—an association of
evil-doers or an association of enemies of the public
good). What we know as freedom of speech and
expression would, in my opinion, be better designated
by the term freedom of investigation and discussion.
Such freedom has a strictly political value, because it is
necessary to the common effort to augment and diffuse
the true and the good in the community. Freedom of
investigation is a fundamental natural right, for man's

---

[43] [See the *Déclaration des droits internationaux de l'homme*
("Declaration of the international rights of man") of the
Institute of International Law, New York, 12 October 1929.]

very nature is to seek the truth. Freedom to spread ideas which one holds to be true corresponds to an aspiration of nature, but like freedom of association it is subject to the regulations of positive law. For it is not true that every thought as such, and because of the mere fact that it was born in a human intellect, has the right to be spread about in the community. The latter has the right to resist the propagation of lies or calumnies; to resist those activities which have as their aim the corruption of morals; to resist those which have as their aim the destruction of the State and of the foundations of common life. Censorship and police methods are, in my opinion, the worst way—at least in peace-time—to insure this repression. But many better ways are possible, not to mention that spontaneous pressure of the common conscience and of public opinion, which spring from the national ethos when it is firmly established. In any event I am convinced that a democratic society is not necessarily an unarmed society, which the enemies of liberty may calmly lead to the slaughterhouse in the name of liberty. Precisely because it is a commonwealth of free men, it must defend: itself with particular energy against those who, out of principle, refuse to accept, and who even work to destroy the foundations of common life in such a regime, the foundations which are liberty and co-operation and mutual civic respect. What here distinguishes a society of free men from a despotic society is that this restriction of the destructive liberties takes place, in a society of free men, only with the institutional guarantees of justice and law.

In my opinion this problem of the effective defence of liberty against those who take advantage of liberty for the purpose of destroying it can be properly solved only by a recasting of society on an organic and pluralist basis. And this presumes, also, that we are dealing with a regime no longer based on the self-propagating power of money and of the symbols of possession, but on the human value and aim of work, where the class struggle, introduced by capitalistic economy, will have been surmounted along with this economy itself, and which will be based alike on the social rights of the working person and the political rights of the civic person.

III. The Rights of the Working Person

Thus we arrive at a third category of rights: the rights of the social person, more particularly of the working person. Generally speaking, a new age of civilization will be called upon to recognize and define the rights of the human being in his social, economic and cultural functions—producers' and consumers' rights, technicians' rights, rights of those who devote themselves to labour of the mind. But the most urgent problems are concerned with the rights of the human being as he is engaged in the function of labour.

Progress in organization and progress in consciousness—these two are simultaneous. I should like to repeat here what I have already pointed out in another book.[44] The principal phenomenon in this point of view, which emerged in the nineteenth century, is the *consciousness of self* (*prise de conscience*), achieved by the working person and the working community. While affecting economic life and the temporal order, this advance is primarily of a spiritual and moral order, and that is what gives it its importance. It is the grasp of consciousness of an offended and humiliated human

---

[44] *True Humanism.* [*Integral Humanism*]

dignity and of the mission of the working world in modern history. It signifies the ascension towards liberty and personality, taken in their inner reality and their social expression, of a community of persons, of the community which is at once nearest to the material bases of human life and the most sacrificed—the community of manual work, the community of human persons charged with this labour.

In a word, this historic gain is the consciousness of the dignity of work and of the worker, of the dignity of the human person in the worker as such.

Let us now glance at one of the consequences of this awareness. If the proletariat demands to be treated as an adult person, by this very fact it is not to be succoured, *ameliorated* or saved by another social class. On the contrary, the principal role in the next phase of evolutions belongs to it and to its own historical upward movement.[45] It is not, however, by withdrawing from the rest of the community in order to exercise a class dictatorship, as Marxism would have it, that the workers and peasants will be in a position to play this inspiring and renewing rôle. It is by organizing and educating themselves, by becoming aware of their responsibilities in the community, and by uniting in their task all the elements, to whatever class they may belong, who have determined to work with them for human liberty.

By the same token we perceive more clearly how the rights of labour have been disengaged in the common consciousness and continue to take shape. First of all there is the right to a just wage, for man's work is not a piece of merchandise subject to the mere law of supply and demand; the wage which it yields must enable the

---

[45] *True Humanism*, pp. 228-229. [*Integral Humanism*, pp. 234-235.]

worker and his family to have a sufficiently human standard of living, in relation to the normal conditions of a given society. Human law will doubtless acknowledge other rights to labour as the economic system becomes transformed. Only by means of a profound recasting of this system can the right to work, the right of every one to find work which will afford a living for himself and his family, become realizable in actual fact; as men become aware of this right, it will assume a powerful force of social transformation.

To cite a particular instance, there is reason to believe that in those types of enterprise where it will be possible, a system of joint ownership and of joint management will replace the wage system, and that with the progress of economic organization a new right will disengage itself for the technically and socially qualified worker: the right to what may be called *the worker's title*, which assures a man that his employment is rightly his, is juridically linked to his person, and that his operative activity will have room to progress in his field. We may rest assured that after the present war, which represents a revolutionary world crisis, social and economic conditions of human life, the systems of property and production will be profoundly and irrevocably changed, and that the present privileges of wealth will in any case give way to a new system of life, better or worse according to whether it is animated by the personalist or the totalitarian spirit. The problem is for thought to be as bold in understanding as the event in striking.

But let us come back to our subject, which is the consideration of the rights of the working person. The rights of the worker as an individual are linked to the rights of the working group, of the trade-unions and of other vocational groups, and the first of these rights is freedom to organize. This freedom—the freedom of workers to group themselves in trade-unions of their choice, the autonomy of the trade-unions themselves, free to confederate as they see fit, without the State having the right to unify them by force or to regiment them, their freedom to make use of those natural weapons which the law grants them, in particular the right to strike (except in the case of a national emergency)—this freedom springs from the natural right of association sanctioned by positive law, and it is the normal condition of the movement of transformation from which a new economic organization will emerge.

What is involved in all this is the sense of the dignity of work, which I mentioned above, the feeling for the rights of the human person in the worker, the rights in the name of which the worker stands before his employer in a relationship of justice and as an adult person, not as a child or as a servant. There is here an essential datum which far surpasses every problem of merely economic and social technique, for it is a *moral* datum, affecting man in his spiritual depth. If it were not built upon this foundation of the rights and dignity of the working person, trade-union or co-operative organization would, in its turn, run the risk of becoming tyranny.

With regard to today's events, it must be noted that, amidst the ruins accumulated by the war, a new phenomenon is taking place, particularly in England and among the Frenchmen who, in and out of France, continue to fight for freedom. It seems that many socialists and many Christians are in process of revising and renewing their social concepts, and at the same time, of getting nearer to one another. Here each one of us must be on his guard against certain temptations which arise from the thinking habits of the past.

The temptation which arises from old socialist concepts is that of granting primacy to economic technique, and by the same token of tending to entrust everything to the power of the State, administrator of the welfare of all, and to its scientific and bureaucratic machinery; which obviously, whether we will or no, leads in the direction of a totalitarianism with a technocratic base. It is not this sort of rationalism of mathematical organization which ought to inspire the work of reconstruction, but rather a practical and experimental wisdom attentive to human ends and means. Thus the idea of planned economy should be replaced by a new idea, based upon the progressive adjustment due to the activity and the reciprocal tension of the autonomous agencies grouping producers and consumers from the bottom up; in such a case it would be better to say adjusted economy than planned economy. Likewise, the idea of 'collectivisation' should be replaced by that of 'associative' ownership of the means of production, or of joint ownership of the enterprise. Aside from certain areas of altogether general interest, whose transformation into public services is to be expected, it is an associative system substituting, as far as possible, joint ownership for the wage system, that, in such a conception and in what above all concerns the industrial level, ought to take the place of the capitalist regime. The working personnel would thus participate in the management of the undertaking, for which, from another point of view, modern technical progress allows the hope of a certain decentralization. When I speak of the associative form of industrial ownership, I am thinking of an *association of persons* (management-technicians, workers, investors) entirely different from the associations of capital which the idea of joint ownership might suggest under the present regime. And I am thinking of an association of persons in which the joint ownership of the private enterprise, itself enmeshed in an organized "community of labour," would be the guarantee of the "worker's title" which we discussed above, and would have as its result the formation and the development of a common patrimony.[46] [...]

It is because the political sphere possesses authority over the economic sphere that the State must control and direct the policy of the supreme national economic agencies, in so far as this policy affects the national totality as such, and in so far as it is linked to the international economic life, which in the world of tomorrow will necessarily be an organized life. The political life and organization of the State affect the common life of human persons and their direction towards a common task, which assumes the strength, peace and harmony of the social body, and which must aim at the conquest of freedom and the establishment of a brotherly city as its supreme ideal; they are of an order superior to the life and organization of economic groups. The political structure of the State implies at its base, as I pointed out in the preceding section, the recognition of the rights of the human person to political life. It must be based on the political rights and liberties of the citizen. The political life of the State

---

[46] Cf. *True Humanism*, pp. 181-183. [*Integral Humanism*, pp. 187-190.] On the level of agricultural production other questions arise. Whatever part industrialization may be called upon to play here, this part would have to remain secondary. In the status to be envisaged, private ownership of the means of production would have to remain centred upon family economy, and co-operative organization and machinism itself would have to be channeled for the benefit of this economy.

must express the thought and the will of the citizen, with regard to the common good and to the common task, which are of an order, not merely material, but principally moral and truly human. It is normal for groups, trade-unions, economic institutions, vocational bodies to have regular means for making their opinion heard, in other words, to play a *consultative* rôle. It is not for them to direct political life or to constitute the political structure of the nation.

In opposition to the totalitarian principle and to all the perversions which it entails, the new conceptions of which I am speaking will have to emphasize the fundamental value of the *pluralist* principle. This principle extends to the entire field of political and social life; in particular, we may count upon it for a reasonable solution of the school problem and the problem of the harmonious dwelling together of various spiritual families, with their specific moral conceptions, in the bosom of the temporal community. In the economic order it lays the foundation not only for that autonomy of groups and associations which we discussed a few minutes ago, but also for the diversity of regime of organization which is suitable to the various typical structures of economic life, in particular, to the structures of industrial economy and to those of agricultural economy.

Lastly, to what does this too-imperfectly sketched outline of the rights of the working person, and of the rights of the groups and communities of which he is a part, correspond, unless it is to the idea of a democratic evolution of working conditions, not carried over from the methods of dialectic conflict and paralysing irresponsibility which existed before the war, but rather inspired by the directive ideas of a new organic and pluralist democracy?

It is fitting for us to come back and examine more closely, as a conclusion to this study, one of the fundamental rights mentioned in this chapter, the right of every human being to personal liberty, or the right to direct his own life as his own master, responsible before God and the law of the community. Such a right is a natural right, but it concerns so profoundly the radical aspirations of the person and the dynamism which they entail that all of human history would not be too long for it to develop completely. It implies the condemnation of slavery and forced labour, particularly as the right to personal liberty takes the more specialized form of the right freely to choose one's work,[47] which corresponds to everyone's obligation to carry his part of the burden of the community. However, the greatest thinkers of Antiquity had not dreamed of condemning slavery, and the medieval theologians considered only slavery in its absolute form as opposed to natural law, where the body and the life of the slave and his primary human rights, like the freedom to marry, are at the mercy of the master.

That is because two factors—on the one hand, the material and technical conditions of work here on earth, and on the other hand, the obstacles suffered by spiritual energies in collective life—grievously, and in the manner of a punishment, thwart the normal development of the fundamental right in question. This right is not merely opposed to slavery in its strict sense, it also involves an aspiration or a wish opposed to servitude in its most general sense, that is to say, opposed to that form of authority of one man over another in which the one who is directed is not directed towards the *common good* by the official charged with

---

[47] [note omitted]

this duty, but is at the service of the *particular* good of the one who is doing the directing, thus alienating his own activity and giving over to another the benefit (the fruit of his activity) which should rightly be his, in other words, becoming to that extent the organ of another person. And it is quite clear that servitude in this sense can take on other shapes than that of slavery in its strict meaning, for instance the form of serfdom or that of the proletariat, and still other forms. These diverse forms of servitude, linked to the conditions of human labour, have been, are being, and will be eliminated only gradually, as the techniques of production and of social life become perfected and as spiritual energies become liberated within communal life. The technical changes introduced into modern economy by the machine can here play a more important and more decisive rôle than did the substitution of animal traction for human traction in the past. If man's reason is strong enough to surmount the formidable crisis provoked in human history by the tremendous power of the techniques of machinism, it will be able to bring forth a new liberation, a better regime, which will mark the end of certain forms of servitude, but this new regime will still be far from freeing human labour from every form, of servitude.

With regard to natural law, absolute bondage thus appears as opposed to natural law considered in its primary requirements, and the other more or less attenuated forms of servitude as opposed to natural law considered in its more or less secondary requirements or yearnings, and in the dynamism which it enfolds. This dynamism will be fully gratified only when every form of servitude shall have disappeared—under the 'new heavens' of the resurrection.

In the meantime, not only must all progress in the diminution of servitude be considered consistent with natural law, but men whose condition of labour still leaves them in some sort of servitude must have a compensating means of protecting their rights as human persons. That is one of the functions of the organization of workers within a capitalist regime. Whatever the form of the new regime, this function should continue to be exerted, particularly in those economic sections where the wage system will still be in force. In a system of organic economy it is possible, moreover, that those individuals who, for one reason or another, will remain outside the pale of trade-unions and working communities, or will not have access to the guarantees and advantages offered by these unions, will constitute a mass exposed to pauperism. They must get help and protection, and organize to defend their right to work.

Lastly, the law which spurs human work to free itself from servitude is not the only one to be considered. Emancipation of human life from physical suffering corresponds to other rights of the human person which the multiple forms of social service and old age security are destined to guarantee—and will doubtless guarantee better if these institutions are of a pluralist type (reducing though not excluding the role of the State) than if they are of a State-dominated type. And an even profounder law requires that all men, in so far as they are coheirs of the common good, should freely have a part in the elementary goods, both material and spiritual, of civilization, to the extent that the community and its organic groups can give their use *free of charge*[48] to human persons who make up this civilization, helping them in this manner to free

---

[48] Cf. *True Humanism*, p. 186 [*Integral Humanism*, p. 192]

themselves from the necessities of matter and go forward in the life of reason and virtue. Thus this chapter concludes with the same considerations as the preceding chapter. The thwarted progress of humanity moves in the direction of human emancipation, not only in the political order but also in the economic and social order, in such a way that the diverse forms of servitude which place one man in the service of another man for the particular good of the latter and as an organ of the latter, may be abolished by degrees, as human history approaches its term. This supposes not only the transition to better states of organization, but also the transition to a better awareness of the dignity of the human person in each of us, and of the primacy of brotherly love amid all the values of our life. In this manner we shall advance towards the conquest of freedom.

To the extent that an authentic reconstruction will emerge from the mortal trial through which the world is passing today, it will have to establish itself upon the affirmation, the recognition and the victory of all the freedoms, spiritual freedom, political freedom, social and working freedom. And it is really and truly by putting our trust in the people—this people which solidly gives its labour and its suffering and, in case of need, its blood—that we may hope to see an authentic reconstruction emerge from the ruins. It is in communion with the people that civilization will find its last chance.

IV. Résumé of the Rights Enumerated

We have not discussed in this study the rights concerned with the international order, whose consideration belongs to a special field, and among which the most important are the right of each State, large or small, to freedom and respect for its autonomy, the right to the respecting of solemn oaths and the sanctity of treaties, the right to peaceful development (a right which, being valid for all, requires for its own development the establishment of an international community having juridical power, and the development of federative forms of organization). It may not be altogether unnecessary at this point to make a summary list of those rights of which we have spoken.

Rights of the human person as such. —The right to existence. —The right to personal liberty or the right to conduct one's own life as master of oneself and of one's acts, responsible for them before God and the law of the community. —The right to the pursuit of the perfection of rational and moral human life. —The right to the pursuit of eternal life along the path which conscience has recognized as the path indicated by God. —The right of the Church and other religious families to the free exercise of their spiritual activity. —The right of pursuing a religious vocation; the freedom of religious orders and groups. —The right to marry according to one's choice and to raise a family, which will in its turn be assured of the liberties due it; —the right of the family society to respect for its constitution, which is based on natural law, not on the law of the State, and which fundamentally involves the morality of the human being. —The right to keep one's body whole. —The right to property. —Finally, the right of every human being to be treated as a person, not as a thing.

Rights of the civic person. —The right of every citizen to participate actively in political life, and in particular the right of equal suffrage for all. —The right of the people to establish the Constitution of the State and to determine for themselves their form of government. —The right of association, limited only by the juridically recognized necessities of the common good, and in particular the right to form political parties or political schools. —The right of free investigation and discussion (freedom of expression).[49] —Political equality, and the equal right of every citizen to his security and his liberties within the State. —The equal right of every one to the guarantees of an independent judiciary power. —Equal possibility of admission to public employment and free access to the venous professions.

Rights of the social person, and more particularly of the working person. —The right freely to choose his work. —The right freely to form vocational groups or trade-unions. The right of the worker to be considered socially as an adult. —The right of economic groups (trade-unions and working communities) and other social groups to freedom and autonomy. —The right to a just wage. The right to work. And wherever an associative system can be substituted for the wage system the right to joint ownership and joint management of the enterprise, and to the 'worker's title.' —The right to relief, unemployment insurance, sick benefits and social security. —The right to have a part, free of charge, depending on the possibilities of the community, in the elementary goods, both material and spiritual, of civilization.[50]

---

[49] The right of association and the right of free investigation and discussion involve the human person considered simply as such, but they manifest themselves in an especially important manner in the sphere of political life.

[50] [note omitted]

Bibliography

The most comprehensive list of books and articles on Maritain's philosophy and life is found in Jean-Louis Allard and Pierre Germain, *Répertoire bibliographique sur la vie et l'oeuvre de Jacques et Raïssa Maritain*, Ottawa, 1994, 232 p. An exhaustive list of the various editions of Maritain's writings and of their translations can be found in occasional supplementary volumes of the *Cahiers Jacques Maritain*, edited by the Cercle d'Études Jacques et Raïssa Maritain, Kolbsheim, France. The Cercle has also produced the *Oeuvres complètes de Jacques et Raïssa Maritain*, 15 vols., Fribourg (Switzerland): Éditions universitaires, 1982-95.

The publication of a 20 volume set, in English, of *The Collected Works of Jacques Maritain* (general editor, Ralph McInerny) is currently underway under auspices of the University of Notre Dame Press.

Some of Maritain's major work in moral philosophy and on related topics, in addition to that used in this volume, may be found in:

Distinguish to Unite: or, The Degrees of Knowledge. New York: Charles Scribner's Sons, 1959. (Tr. under the supervision of G.B. Phelan)]
An Essay on Christian Philosophy. New York: Philosophical Library, 1955. (Tr. Edward H. Flannery)

Freedom in the Modern World. London: Sheed & Ward, 1935.

Scholasticism and Politics. New York: The Macmillan Company, 1940. [with Mortimer Jerome Adler]

The Twilight of Civilization. London: Sheed and Ward, 1946.

Christianity and Democracy. New York: Scribner's 1944. (Tr. Doris C. Anson)

Principes d'une politique humaniste, New York: Éditions de la maison française, 1944.

Pour la justice. New York: Éditions de la maison française, 1945.

The Person and the Common Good. New York: Charles Scribner's Sons, 1947. (Tr. John J. Fitzgerald)

An Introduction to Basic Problems of Moral Philosophy. Albany, NY: Magi Books, 1990.

Le Philosophie dans la cité. Paris: Alsatia, 1960.

Moral Philosophy. London: G. Bles, 1964. (Tr. and Ed. Joseph W. Evans)

Some major studies of Maritain's work are:

Allard, Jean-Louis. *Education for Freedom: The Philosophy of Education of Jacques Maritain.* Notre Dame, IN: University of Notre Dame Press, 1982.

Allard, Jean-Louis (ed.). *Jacques Maritain, Philosophe dans la Cité / A Philosopher in the World.* Ottawa: University of Ottawa Press, 1985.

American Maritain Association. *Selected Papers from the Conference—Seminar on Jacques Maritain's The Degrees of Knowledge.* St. Louis: American Maritain Association, 1981.

Armour, Leslie. "Maritain and the Metaphysics of Community," *Maritain Studies / Études Maritain-iennes,* Vol. 3 (1987): 53-81.

Armour, Leslie. "Gewirth, Maritain, and MacIntyre: the Unity and Universalization of Moral Principle," *Maritain Studies / Études maritainennes*, Vol. 7 (1991): 49-78.

Bars, Henry. *Maritain en notre temps.* Paris: Bernard Grasset, 1959.

Bars, Henry. *La politique selon Jacques Maritain.* Paris: Éditions ouvrières, 1961.

Cauchy, Venant. "A Defence of Natural Ethics," *Proceedings of the American Catholic Philosophical Association*, Vol. XXIX (1955): 206-18.

Cooper, John W. "Democratic Pluralism and Human Rights: the Political Theologies of Jacques Maritain and Reinhold Niebuhr," *Jacques Maritain, Philosophe dans la Cité / A Philosopher in the World*, (ed.) Jean-Louis Allard, Ottawa: University of Ottawa Press, 1985, pp. 327-36.

Cooper, John W. "Natural Law and Economic Humanism," *Jacques Maritain: The Man and His Metaphysics.* [Volume IV of *Études maritainiennes / Maritain Studies*], (ed.) John F. X. Knasas, Mishawaka, IN: American Maritain Association, 1988.

Croteau, Jacques. *Les fondements thomistes du personnalisme de Maritain.* Ottawa: Éditions de l'Université d'Ottawa, 1950.

Daly, Mary F. *Natural Knowledge of God in the Philosophy of Jacques Maritain.* Rome: Officium Libri Catholici - Catholic Book Agency, 1966.

Dewan, Lawrence. "St Thomas, Our Natural Lights, and the Moral Order," *Angelicum*, Vol. LXVII: (1990) 285-307.

DiJoseph, John. *Jacques Maritain and the Moral Foundation of Democracy.* Lanham, MD: Rowman & Littlefield, 1996.

Doering, Bernard. *Jacques Maritain and the French Catholic Intellectuals.* Notre Dame, IN: University of Notre Dame Press, 1983.

Dunaway, John M. *Jacques Maritain.* Boston: Twayne Publishers, G. K. Hall and Co., 1978.

Evans, Joseph W. (ed.), *Jacques Maritain: The Man and His Achievement.* New York: Sheed and Ward, 1963.

Evans, Joseph W. *Jacques Maritain (1882-1973): A Biographical Memoir.* Washington, D.C.: National Academy of Education, 1973.

Evans, Joseph W. "Jacques Maritain and the Problem of Pluralism in Political Life," *The Review of Politics*, Vol. XXII (1960): 307-23

Fecher, Charles A. *The Philosophy of Jacques Maritain.* Westminster, MD.: Newman Press, 1953.

Floucat, Yves. *Pour une philosophie chretienne: eléments d'un débat fondamental.* Paris: Téqui, 1983.

Gallagher, Donald and Idella. *The Achievement of Jacques and Raissa Maritain: A Bibliography.* New York: Doubleday and Co., 1962.

Gurian, Waldemar. "On Maritain's Political Philosophy," *The Thomist*, Vol. V (1943): 7-22.

Haggerty, Donald F. *Jacques Maritain and the Notion of Connaturality.* (Doctoral thesis in moral theology, Pontifical Lateran University) Rome: Academia Alfonsiana, 1995.

Hubert, Bernard and Yves Floucat, editors. *Jacques Maritain et ses contemporains.* Paris: Desclée, 1991.

Hudson, Deal W. and Matthew J. Mancini, editors. *Understanding Maritain: Philosopher and Friend.* Macon, Georgia: Mercer University Press, 1987.

Institut International Jacques Maritain. International Jacques Maritain Institute. *Droits des Peuples, Droits de l'Homme.* Paris: Éditions du Centurion, 1984.

Jung, Hwa Yol. *The Foundation of Jacques Maritain's Political Philosophy.* Gainesville, Florida: University of Florida Press, 1960.

Killoran, John B., "Maritain's Critique of Liberalism," *Notes et documents*, n.s., No. 21-22 (1988): 110-22.

Knight, F.H. "The Rights of Man and Natural Law: Discussion," *Ethics*, Vol. LIV (1944): 124-45.

Knight, F.H. "Natural Law: Last Refuge of the Bigot," *Ethics*, Vol. LIX (1949): 127-35.

Knasas, John F. X. (ed.). *Jacques Maritain: The Man and His Metaphysics.* [Volume IV of *Études maritainiennes / Maritain Studies*] Mishawaka, IN: American Maritain Association, 1988.

Lynch, Lawrence. "Jacques Maritain: Some Significant Aspects of his Moral and Social Philosophy," *Notes et documents*, n.s., No. 9-10 (1985): 118-30.

Maritain Centenary. *The Review of Politics*, Vol. 44, October, No. 4, 1982.

Maritain Studies / Études maritainennes, Vol. XII (1996), Thematic issue on "Maritain and the Natural Law / Maritain et la loi naturelle"

The Maritain Volume of *The Thomist.* New York: Sheed and Ward, 1943.

McInerny, Ralph. *Art and Prudence: Studies in the Thought of Jacques Maritain.* Notre Dame, IN: University of Notre Dame Press, 1988.

Michener, Norah Willis. *Maritain on the Nature of Man in a Christian Democracy.* Hull (Canada): Éditions "L'Eclair", 1955.

Minkiel, Stephen J., C.M. (ed.). *Jacques Maritain: The Man for Our Times.* Erie, PA: Gannon University Press, 1981.

Nelson, Ralph. "Nature and Adventure," *Maritain Studies / Études maritainennes*, Vol. 7 (1991): 5-26.

Nottingham, William J. *Christian Faith and Secular Action: An Introduction to the Life and Thought of Jacques Maritain.* St. Louis: The Bethany Press, 1968.

Papini, Roberto (ed.). *Jacques Maritain e la Società Contemporanea.* Milan: Massimo, 1978.

Possenti, Vittorio, editor. *Jacques Maritain: Oggi.* Milan: Vita e Pensiero, 1983.

Possenti, Vittorio (ed). *Maritain e Marx.* Milan: Massimo, 1978.

Ramsey, Paul. *Nine Modern Moralists.* Englewood Cliffs, N.J.: Prentice-Hall, 1962.

Redpath, Peter A. (ed.) *From Twilight to Dawn: The Cultural Vision of Jacques Maritain.* Mishawaka, IN: American Maritain Association, 1990.

Sweet, William. "Maritain's Criticisms of Natural Law Theories," *Études maritainiennes / Maritain Studies* Vol. XII (1996): 33-49.

Sweet, William. "Maritain, Jacques," *Stanford Encyclopedia of Philosophy* (ed.) Edward N. Zalta. Stanford, CA, 1998. http://plato.stanford.edu/entries/maritain/

Sweet, William. "Solidarity and Human Rights," *Philosophical Theory and the Universal Declaration of Human Rights,* (ed.) William Sweet. Ottawa, ON: University of Ottawa Press, 2003.

Torre, Michael D. (ed.) *Freedom in the Modern World: Jacques Maritain, Yves R. Simon, Mortimer J. Adler.* Mishawaka, IN: American Maritain Association, 1990.

Index